Library of
Davidson College

Growing Up in the James Family
Henry James, Sr., as Son and Father

Research in Clinical Psychology, No. 14

Peter E. Nathan, Series Editor

Henry and Anna Starr Professor of Psychology
Chairman, Department of Clinical Psychology
Rutgers, the State University of New Jersey

Other Titles in This Series

No. 6	*Coping with Chemotherapy*	Karin E. Ringler
No. 7	*Adolescent Suicidal Behavior: A Family Systems Model*	Roma J. Heillig
No. 8	*The Divorce Experience of Working and Middle Class Women*	Toni L'Hommedieu
No. 9	*Climbing the Ladder of Success in Highheels: Backgrounds of Professional Women*	Jill A. Steinberg
No. 10	*Work and Marriage: The Two-Profession Couple*	Roslyn K. Malmaud
No. 11	*Families of Gifted Children*	Dewey G. Cornell
No. 12	*The Legacy of the Holocaust: Psychohistorical Themes in the Second Generation*	Robert M. Prince
No. 13	*The First Pregnancy: An Integrating Principle in Female Psychology*	Jellemieke C. Hees-Stauthamer

Growing Up in the James Family

Henry James, Sr., as Son and Father

by
Katherine Weissbourd

UMI RESEARCH PRESS
Ann Arbor, Michigan

Copyright © 1985, 1978
Katherine Allison Weissbourd
All rights reserved

Produced and distributed by
UMI Research Press
an imprint of
University Microfilms International
A Xerox Information Resources Company
Ann Arbor, Michigan 48106

Library of Congress Cataloging in Publication Data

Weissbourd, Katherine.
Growing up in the James family.

(Research in clinical psychology ; no. 14)
Bibliography: p.
Includes index.
"A revision of the author's dissertation, Northwestern University, 1978"—T.p. verso.
 1. Identity (Psychology) in children—Case studies.
2. Identity (Psychology)—Case studies. 3. Fathers and sons—Case studies. 4. Erikson, Erik H. (Erik Homburger), 1902-   . 5. James, Henry, 1811-1882.
6. James, William, 1842-1910. I. Title. II. Series.
[DNLM: James, Henry, 1811-1882. 2. James, William, 1842-1910. 3. James family. 4. Famous Person—biography. 5. Psychology—history.
W1 RE227FD no. 14 / WZ 100 J277W]
BF723.I56W44   1985   155.2'092'2 [B]   84-29779
ISBN 0-8357-1652-X (alk. paper)

To Burt

Religious feeling is thus an absolute addition to the Subject's range of life. It gives him a new sphere of power. When the outward battle is lost, and the outer world disowns him, it redeems and vivifies an interior world which otherwise would be an empty waste.

William James,
The Varieties of Religious Experience

Henry James, Sr., with William's son, Henry James III, c. 1879–80

Contents

List of Illustrations   *xi*

Introduction   *1*

1   Erikson's Psychohistorical Theory   *3*
    Psychohistory
    Identity
    The Sponsoring Relationship
    Conclusion

2   The James Family, 1789–1860   *13*
    William of Albany's American Success
    Henry's Early Childhood
    The Financial and Spiritual Inheritance
    Marriage and Early Family Years
    Europe

3   Father's Ideas   *49*
    The Inner World
    Self-Expression
    Society and the Self
    The Experience of Relationships

4   Resolving the Philosophical Conflict between William and Henry   *63*
    Science and Philosophy
    Accepting a Scientific Universe
    Religious Conversion
    William's Acceptance of Henry's Identity

Illustrations   *85*

Bibliography   *117*

Index   *119*

List of Illustrations

Frontispiece. Henry James, Sr., with William's son, Henry James III, c. 1879-80
(By permission of the Houghton Library, Harvard University)

Following page 83

1. North Pearl Street, Albany and the North Dutch Church from the corner of Columbia Street looking north, c. 1805-10
   From an original sketch by James Eights
   (By permission from the Collection of McKinney Library, Albany Institute of History and Art)

2. North Pearl Street (west side), Albany from Maiden Lane north, as it was in 1814
   From original sketches by James Eights
   (By permission from the Collection of McKinney Library, Albany Institute of History and Art)

3. State Street, Albany, 1837
   (By permission from the Collection of McKinney Library, Albany Institute of History and Art)

4. William James of Albany, c. 1810
   (By permission of the Houghton Library, Harvard University)

5. Henry James, Sr., c. 1873-78
   Photograph by Balch
   (By permission of the Houghton Library, Harvard University)

List of Illustrations

6. Mary James, c. 1880
   (By permission of the Houghton Library, Harvard University)

7. William James at 18, c. 1860
   (By permission of the Houghton Library, Harvard University)

8. William James in Brazil, 1865
   (By permission of the Houghton Library, Harvard University)

9. William James at about 24, c. 1866
   (By permission of the Houghton Library, Harvard University)

10. Pencil sketch of himself by William James, c. 1866
    (By permission of the Houghton Library, Harvard University)

11. William James, 1903
    Photograph by Notman
    (By permission of the Houghton Library, Harvard University)

12. Henry James, Jr., and William James, c. 1900
    (By permission of the Houghton Library, Harvard University)

13. Henry James, Jr., and William James, c. 1905
    (By permission of the Houghton Library, Harvard University)

14. Alice James, 1870
    (By permission of the Houghton Library, Harvard University)

15. Robertson James, 1872
    (By permission of the Houghton Library, Harvard University)

16. Garth Wilkinson James, c. 1873
    (By permission of the Houghton Library, Harvard University)

Introduction

Attempts to apply psychological understanding to biography frequently result in an approach that is overly clinical. The reader is left with an uncomfortable sense that the author has placed the subject on the couch without the subject's consent and even before it has been determined that treatment is called for. Hopefully, the developing field of psychohistory can provide a format in which it is possible to look at a person's development, including his or her times of unhappiness, without coming to the foredrawn conclusion that there is a neurosis or a destructive parental figure lurking in the background.

In this study of the James family, E. H. Erikson's work provides a theoretical tool for understanding the conflicts that arose between Henry James, Sr., and his father, and re-emerged between Henry and his oldest son William. Identity formation and sponsorship, as they are described by Erikson, will be used to clarify ways in which the conflicts contributed to the overall development of both men. Erikson sees fathers as playing a primary role in personal development and in the integration of the child into adult society:

> Fathers, it appears, were there before we were, they were strong when we were weak, they saw us before we saw them; not being mothers . . . they love us differently, more dangerously. Here, I think, is the origin of an idea attested to by myths, dreams, and symptoms, namely that the fathers (as some animal fathers do) could have annihilated us before we became strong enough to appear as their rivals. . . . Thus, we owe our fathers two lives; one by way of conception (which even the most enlightened children can visualize only very late in childhood); the other by way of a voluntary sponsorship, of a *paternal* love. (Erikson 1958, 123-24)

In the first chapter of this study, Erikson's work on identity formation and sponsorship is discussed. The second chapter presents the history of the James family from Henry's early childhood through William's early adulthood. Henry's writing and its psychological implications provide the focus of the third chapter. This is followed by an examination of Henry's conflicts with William over philosophy, and the influence of those conflicts on the relationship between the two men.

The James family story conveys the intensity of Henry's paternal love as it played against his equally extreme devotion to his mental life. This was the inner drama that set the stage for an intense and remarkable family life, so remarkable that it produced William James the psychologist and philosopher and Henry James the novelist.

1
Erikson's Psychohistorical Theory

Psychohistory

Psychohistory is the application of the methods and concepts of dynamic psychology to events and individuals of historical importance. Rapaport has defined dynamic psychology as:

> attempting to do justice both to the forces which impinge upon the individual and to the physiological and psychological (conscious and unconscious) forces and regulative mechanisms which determine the individual's functioning within this environment. ([1966] 1967, 290)

The complexities of psychohistory are focused by this broad definition of dynamic psychology. When human experience is taken as the focus of study, as in the case of psychohistory, the scholar becomes particularly attuned to how little can be said with absolute certainty. The patterns that emerge after a prolonged study of an individual or an event in history rarely reflect clearly demarcated processes. Most events are the products of many variables which exert subtle degrees of influence over people's decisions and activities. The psychohistorian hopes to do justice to his or her subjects by alerting the reader to the kinds of experiences that appear to have affected the crucial decisions which they have made. These experiences frequently include painful and exciting events, intense feelings, important expectations, and characteristic activities. These experiences are often influenced by interchanges with the community in which the person lives.

Anyone acquainted with psychohistorical research can testify to its demands and to the abundance of simplistic and narrow studies. The difficulties of devising a theory that encompasses both individual development and cultural patterns of relationships and values have discouraged most researchers from theoretical speculation. The predominant tendency in psychohistory is to choose a topic of interest and to apply what little one is able to understand rather than to attempt to develop broad theoretical concepts.

The abundance of available historical material in contrast to the scarcity of psychosocial theory has reinforced this trend.

What can be found in the psychohistorical literature is a loose organization of relatively independent studies. They might be characterized, as Kai Erikson has suggested in regard to communities, as depicting "not just the *core values* to which people pay homage but also the *lines of point and counterpoint* along which they diverge" (1976, 82). The result is likely to give the psychohistorian a sense of urban sprawl, or perhaps of an academic gold rush.

In the absence of clearly delineated boundaries, it is difficult to know at exactly what point history, psychology, criticism, fiction, clinical description, and biography enter the field of psychohistory. One deals rather with a clustering phenomenon, a general interest in dynamic psychology which has not yet been synthesized into any single theoretical system. The importance of dynamic psychology for psychohistory is that it provides some sense of core values and thus gives direction to those who pursue this area of interest.

Dynamic psychology has developed through the ego psychology of Hartmann and Erikson. Rapaport ([1954] 1967, [1956] 1967, [1958] 1967) has shown the interrelationships between these two thinkers. Hartmann (1939) first presented a theory that related individual developmental processes to cultural expectations, but did not develop this notion beyond a general formulation.

Erikson moved beyond Hartmann by devising a more specific interactional theory of developmental processes. Rapaport ([1956] 1967) notes that Erikson utilizes the concepts of sequence, interaction, and mutuality to describe how social and individual development influence the way in which personalities are formed. His model is a phase-specific presentation of the entire life cycle in which particular developmental tasks must be accomplished by the individual, with help from family or society, at particular ages. The successful resolution of these tasks requires coordination among members of the society. An interlocking of the stages of the participants takes place according to cultural norms and patterns; for example, the developmental tasks of childhood are influenced by the parents' ability to undertake caretaking responsibilities and the cultural attitudes toward children. As individuals resolve these tasks, their solutions become integrated as socially valued activities unless they are rejected as unsuitable.

Rapaport presents Erikson's concept of identity as an example of the interaction of personal and cultural capacities. He correctly characterizes identity formation as resembling other developmental stages in that it requires a functional "interlocking" of identifications, skills, and social conventions ([1956] 1967, 608). From his perspective as an ego psychologist, identity formation is a crucial stage of development that presents frequent conflict and is of clinical importance.

For the psychohistorian, identity is a more pivotal concept. The family serves as the child's main source of information about his or her social world. Identity formation involves moving outside one's family of origin and seeking a role as an adult in one's culture. This is one point at which psychohistory and ego psychology converge. Ego psychology must incorporate an understanding of the young person's encounter with the culture. Psychohistory must integrate a developmental theory of personality into its focus on historical process.

At the same time this convergence gives rise to two distinct images of personality. The predominant trend in psychohistory (de Mause 1974; Demos 1970; Hunt 1970), as well as psychoanalytic ego psychology (Gedo and Goldberg 1973; Jacobson 1964; Schafer 1968), has been to retain a primary focus on the child and family dynamics and a secondary focus on the culture. From this perspective the culture influences the family, which determines the predominant characteristics forming the child's identity. Early identifications are regarded as arising from the child's milieu and as largely inaccessible to alteration in later social environments.

The alternative image, found in Erikson and applied in this study, is one in which identity and social relationships are seen as developmental extensions of early identifications. While early childhood experience is retained as a crucial factor in adult experience, choices, and beliefs, it is by no means regarded as a limiting factor. Experiences of adolescence and adulthood are as crucial as those of early childhood in influencing the ways in which identifications, skills, and social inventions are synthesized into a sense of identity. Erikson has arrived at an original conceptual understanding of this psychohistorical matrix. This book uses his theoretical constructs but focuses on interpersonal themes rather than the individual's life cycle.

This image of the relationship between the person and his or her social world calls for an integration of what traditionally have been competitive views of personal and cultural history. Lifton has stated:

> Much of the intellectual impulse of psychoanalysis has been toward extracting man's psychological self *from* the historical process, to be seen independently of it; and much of the intellectual impulse of history (as a discipline) has been toward depicting an amalgam of man's sequential group behavior, viewed independently of his individual psychology. Thus we may say — and I exaggerate only slightly — that psychoanalysis seeks to eliminate history; and history seeks to eliminate psychological man. (1965, 295)

According to Erikson's model, historical and personal processes are interactional and cooperative. Neither is taken as an independent variable that causes fluctuation in its complementary dependent variable.

Traditionally the psychologist has placed himself in an experimental field in which he introduces one element in hopes of influencing, in a lawful manner, a second variable. The historian has functioned by actively introducing connections which he hopes will explain historical process in an efficient and meaningful manner (Barzun 1974).

The psychohistorian's method is neither the psychological experimentalist's nor the historical pragmatist's. He suspends himself within a given field of interaction as an observer. As Erikson (1975) has argued, he sustains his observational powers through a mutual awareness of his own and his subjects' environmental fields. From this vantage point he observes the emergence of shared themes (Lifton 1974).

These themes are then integrated into his material in a manner which resembles that of both psychologist and historian. He looks for predictable interactions. If a certain kind of event takes place, such as an intense relationship, he predicts that certain responses will be found. He also imposes in a pragmatic manner the efficient connections that fit his theoretical understanding (Campbell 1969).

The psychohistorical paradigm integrates ego psychology and history through an understanding of both developmental and historical processes. Awareness of the passage of time, the uncertainty of events, and the limited capacities of the individual for rational control over his experience are among the cognitive tools which he applies. These are perhaps the most important guidelines at this stage of psychohistorical knowledge. What remains to be developed and critically evaluated are the themes that serve as pivotal events in personal and historical interactions.

This book focuses on three forms of interaction in Erikson's psychohistorical theory: identity, sponsorship, and historical actuality. These are applied to a pivotal event within the James family: the father-son relationship. Several studies have discussed the importance of the father-son relationship in the Victorian era (Freud [1928] 1963, Strout 1968, Janick and Toulman 1973, Mazlish 1975, Rosenzweig 1943). None, however, have applied the interactional model developed from Erikson's theory.

Identity

In altering the theoretical contributions of psychoanalysis to fit the social and experiential aspects of development, Erikson has devised a paradigm suitable for psychohistory. Following the concepts of the ego psychologists, he incorporates the notions of an active organizing ego, intentional behavior, and the influence of consciousness on mental life. In *Childhood and Society* (1963) Erikson replaces the psychoanalytic notion of a fixed psychic structure with a more flexible model of personality, the life cycle. He sees personality development as a series of transformations in response to particular developmental crises. Identity arises within a particular phase of development as a resolution to the crisis of adolescence.

At adolescence, Erikson argues, childhood ends and the individual begins to see himself in a more active role. He becomes an agent in his image of himself and in his interactions with others. Youths "are now primarily concerned with what they feel they are" (1963, 201), and seek "to integrate all identifications with the vicissitudes of the libido, with the aptitudes developed out of endowment, and with the opportunities offered in social roles" (1963, 261).

Cognitively, the youth can imagine himself as having a place in history. Social relationships and thought processes assume a new dimension as a result of this change, so the youth requires more complex self-imagery. Thinking at this age is equally directed toward self and environment, and toward their mutual influence as interacting entities. This gives rise to the concept of identity, the idea of a self which can influence the environment, and which in turn must respond to social restrictions.

Erikson argues that "psychoanalysis has consistently described the vicissitudes of instincts and of the ego only up to adolescence" (1963, 277) and that his shift in interest reflects a growing focus on the present as a vital part of the person's orientation. The youth becomes particularly concerned with "what he should believe in and who he should—or, indeed, might be or become" (1963, 279). A sense of self develops as means to anticipate certain ends and perhaps bring them about. It is not merely a method of stabilizing present experience in terms of the past.

In *Young Man Luther* (1958), Luther's identity crisis marks the beginning of an historical movement. Severe identity crisis, Erikson argues, may lead to growth in the unusual individual. The stress of becoming an active adult leads the youth to develop new forms of thought and activity.

> Still others, although suffering and deviating dangerously through what appears to be a prolonged adolescence, eventually come to contribute an original bit to an emerging style of life: the very danger which they have sensed has forced them to mobilize capacities to see and say, to dream and plan, to design and construct, in new ways. (1958, 14-15)

Erikson again criticizes the traditional psychoanalytic view of the neurotic individual, in which "facing a problem" is substituted for "facing a face" (1958, 17). The face symbolizes the active and evaluative adult self, and the sense of identity. In contrast, traditional psychoanalysis tends to view the self as a product of the egocentric experiences of childhood. In traditional theory, the individual becomes the passive child who is not, nor can be, the adolescent or adult agent seeking to face, manipulate, and master childhood problems and identifications. Erikson's goals differ from this. He shows that during adolescence "the resources of tradition fuse with new inner resources to create something potentially new: a new person; and with this new person a new generation, and with that, a new era" (1958, 20).

Erikson views thought and action as having a crucial influence on identity. These are explored through Luther's conversion. He also points to the consolidating factors in experience, showing that the social environment supports psychological stability in adult life. When "resources of tradition fuse with new inner resources to create something potentially new: a new person" (1958, 20), the implication is that a sense of identity requires stability in the environment and that the resolution of an identity crisis may require forces of social and cultural change.

Erikson presents Luther's religious conversion as an example of identity consolidation. In situations such as Luther's, in which cultural change is inaugurated by identity choices, the new sense of self arises following a feeling of being overcommitted to what one is not. The youth realizes that he or she is loyal to a world view from which the active self has been excluded, the world of restrictive childhood identifications. He or she must integrate his or her capacity to act on others in ways that are personally meaningful and socially acceptable, even if this involves conflict with predominant cultural values. To some degree, every experience of identity formation includes similar patterns of re-evaluation and reorganization as the developing adult adopts processes through which he or she molds an identity from past identifications.

Erikson develops a correspondence between active identity-forming processes and psychoanalytic concepts. The oral imagery of taking in and spitting out to establish a sense of boundaries corresponds to idealization. In youth, the potential isolation when one rejects an old world is counteracted by feelings of merger and ideological commonality in one's new life. Devotion and commitment are thus important psychological processes in identity formation.

Second, the youth seeks new forms of power and leadership, a phase profoundly linked to issues of obedience and self-control. Here again traditional psychoanalytic themes emerge. These include issues of control and compliance, the appropriateness and likeability of one's productions and activities, and the tension of waiting long enough to be the master of one's actions, yet not so long that they become dangerous to oneself. The wait here is not merely an issue of physiological control but also a question of actively choosing the best possible moment, anticipating one's own capacity to produce and others' capacities to respond.

Perhaps most central to the concept of identity consolidation is the young person's sense of presence or integrity. This includes a mutually adaptive relationship to the social system, a capacity to be direct about oneself to others and to receive an inclusive response. In this dimension of the identity crisis, Erikson introduces the possibility of autonomy and integrity and the threat of aggression too harshly directed against either oneself or some other, prohibitive presence.

Within this context, Erikson introduces the crucial role of the father as a prohibitive or a sponsoring influence. If the father has been sufficiently harsh, self-indulgent, or distant, the youth may reject paternal sponsorship and search for a more acceptable father figure during the identity crisis.

Erikson moves then to a discussion of the process by which identity is reformulated, noting that in Luther's case "he first had to grow into the role which he had usurped without meaning to" (1958, 144). He introduces an image of a supportive sponsor who represents the adult world to the youth. He describes the relationship as an "ambivalent father transference" (1958, 168), which revives all the intense love and hate of earlier identifications. However, these earlier identifications are experienced in more complex ways, with the youth now regarding his own activity as determining the meaningfulness of the relationship.

Erikson explains identity formation as the product of both structural change and new forms of relationships. Intense early childhood relationships and feelings are re-experienced through the sponsoring process, but with an increased sense of responsibility on the part of the youth. He can then begin to transform his personality in accordance with, or in opposition to, historical and cultural expectations.

The Sponsoring Relationship

Erikson argues that the principle of active mastery becomes that of actuality through the development of the sponsoring relationship. In this context, he focuses on dimensions of conflict in that relationship. The youths feel:

> an infantile "account to settle," or what they themselves often refer to as a "curse" to be lived with, or to be lived down. . . . In each case, however, the fathers had tied their sons to themselves in such a way that overt rebellion or hate was impossible. By the same token, they had also imposed on their sons a sense of being both needed and chosen by their fathers, and thus of carrying a superior destiny and duty, although these very sons as children or youths felt isolated or weak, physically inferior or shy and cowardly. (1964, 202–3)

What must be settled is the child's ambivalent attitude toward the sponsoring parent. The child turns to the parent for meaning, a process that the parent actively encourages and in fact demands. During the identity crisis, however, the significance of the sponsor's values must be tested. If they help the youth, they do so in the form of an account to settle, for their importance and trustworthiness must be re-examined in order to preserve their historical suitability. To the extent that the sponsor's value system is not helpful, the inheritance is a curse that the youth must live with or live down.

Erikson extends his image of the sponsoring relationship beyond an image of the sponsor as encouraging active mastery. The tie that binds father to son imposes maturity by preventing overt rebellion in response to what is felt as a paternal curse. The tension that this relationship creates must find outlets. In the parent, compensation is made by conveying a special sense of caring while the child develops a special sense of vulnerability and weakness which he must strive to overcome.

The introspective attitude that develops during adolescence places increased demands on communication. As he becomes aware of his responsibility in relationships, the youth must be more active in denying expression of his immediate impulses. He develops a special sense of vulnerability in which he sees himself as unhappy but as able to act on his own behalf. He adopts an attitude of evaluative ambivalence toward the sponsor in which he tests the sponsor's sense of morality. The issue of taking responsibility raises questions as to whether he might become his own or even his father's sponsor. The process of sponsorship then develops into an interchange, during which the youth tests his capacity to sponsor himself. Young people "indeed, *have* to become their own fathers and in a way their fathers' fathers while not yet adult" (1969, 102).

It is through this free exchange of roles that the process of identity formation continues. The father-son pattern perpetuates itself beyond the paternal relationship and becomes the means of achieving intrapsychic growth and interpersonal closeness. The relationship becomes less focused on ideal images and more responsive to immediate feelings.

The sponsoring relationship engenders a kind of flexibility and a moral commitment to something beyond a firm and whole self. The self must be integrated into a series of active relationships. It is a sense not so much of wholeness as of interaction and communication.

Erikson describes the sponsoring relationship in a way which lends itself to a functional rather than a structural theory of identity and the self. He presents those who resolve their identity crises most creatively as moving beyond their intrapsychic selves to interests in the world at large, expanding the concept of historical actuality to describe the impact of history and personality on each other. Consequently, Erikson creates a kind of boundary between Freudian structural theory and functional theory. As he moves back and forth across this boundary, relationships and distinctions are somewhat blurred. For Erikson, therefore, psychohistory becomes a source of exploration of the new territory of a functional, interactional, and relationship-based approach to personality and history.

Conclusion

Erikson's psychohistorical theory has been presented through his development of two central concepts, identity and sponsorship. Identity begins at adolescence. It is the stage of development in which the person sees himself as an agent on his own behalf who in turn influences others by means of his identity choices.

Sponsorship is a relationship between members of the community and those undergoing identity-forming experiences. It is an interlocking relationship for it aids the community in maintaining flexibility in its boundaries and stabilizes and limits identity resolutions. Sponsorship involves a unique form of identification in which active interchange of roles replaces idealization as the form of communication and development. It is successful when it increases both parties' capacities for responsible action; that is, their ability to work and to care.

Erikson uses the term "historical actuality" to describe the expression and integration of these identity-forming and sponsoring experiences within the community. Communities foster identity formation and historical actuality through an openness to new experiences on the part of community members, a willingness to undergo change in values, and an eventual communication and acceptance of the boundaries and limitations imposed by the tasks which ensure collective survival.

In the course of history these processes form a single unit of shared activity and meaning. Cultural values arise in the form of significant issues, or themes, which must be worked out in relationships involving identity and sponsorship. An identity crisis is a rejection of values that conflict with one's image of oneself as an active, responsible adult. New relationships are sought in which these issues are confronted. The sponsor is initially viewed as a representative of the excluding culture and is ambivalently idealized. The relationship develops into a more open and mutual one through flexibility, caring, and a dedicated willingness to work out the problems of the identity crisis.

In the course of this relationship both parties increase their understanding of what works within their community. The sponsor is confronted with his vision of his world and must assume responsibility for its viability for others as well as himself. He also confronts his capacity to retain a sense of continuity with the identifications and skills of others through his values and activities. When the process succeeds, its net effect is to expand and clarify the values of the community, to reinforce the meaningfulness of finding communal solutions to personal problems, and to satisfy the need for shared human experience. These are the psychohistorical dimensions of the three functions of identity: a positive feeling about one's identifications, a set of skills which enables this feeling to be shared with others, and an experience of one's cultural world as flexible and inclusive. These processes are explored further as they were expressed in the experiences of Henry James, Sr., his father William of Albany, and his son William James.

2
The James Family, 1789–1860

William of Albany's American Success

In 1789 William of Albany arrived in America. The city in which he would make his fortune was described by Jedidiah Morse in a American geography book, published that same year, as follows:

> Albany is said to be an unsocial place. This is naturally to be expected. A heterogeneous collection of people, invested with all their national prejudices, eager in the pursuit of gain, and jealous of a rivalship, cannot expect to enjoy the pleasures of social intercourse or the sweets of an intimate and refined friendship. (Weise 1884, 403)

The attractions of financial gain in Albany did not diminish in the next few years. In 1796 Isaac Weld, Jr., reported that there were "fewer places in America more advantageously situated for commerce" (Munsell 1869, 210). Weld's travels had led him to Albany on the 4th of July.

> A day still fresh in the memory of every American, and which appears so glorious in the annals of their country, would, it might be expected, have called forth more brilliant and more general rejoicings; but the downright phlegmatic people in this neighborhood, intent upon making money, and enjoying the solid advantages of the revolution, are but little disposed to waste their time in what they consider idle demonstrations of joy. (Munsell 1869, 210–11)

William James was 18 when he arrived in America. He became so bound up in its financial milieu that it is impossible to imagine how he might have developed outside of it. His style of relating to others focused on finance, reflecting the predominant mood of the community in which he lived. The little that is known about his move to America raises the issue of his relationship with his father in financial terms.

The circumstances of William of Albany's beginnings in America are the subject of some mystery, for historians report two versions. According to the first of these, William arrived as an impoverished youth, carrying a Latin grammar book and anxious to see the battlefields of the Revolutionary War. The second version of his arrival tells of his father's having come to America first. William followed his father, then became involved in a business transaction which gave him ample funds for beginning a business of his own (Warren 1934, 1-2).

This anecdote is striking because it raises the question of paternal sponsorship within the James family and the American culture. William of Albany may or may not have been a self-made man, despite the readiness with which his later life fits the image. He probably came to be who he was with the help and sponsorship of his father.

There is a further dimension to the family legend which says that William of Albany's father was a minister and that William came to America to escape pressure to follow in his father's footsteps. This suggests a second familiar theme, of conflict in the relationship between father and son. Whatever difficulties and supports there were, they were intense enough to motivate William of Albany to remain in America and devote his life to the task of creating a financial empire over which he exerted extreme control.

Once settled, William of Albany quickly gravitated toward the developing American business ideology. He settled in Albany, New York, in 1793 at age 22. For two years he worked as a store clerk then went into business with a partner selling tobacco and "segars." Two years later he opened a grocery and dry goods store. The following year he built a tobacco factory. Expansions continued, including an express business, a salt works, and land purchases.

William of Albany prospered particularly during and immediately following the War of 1812. Underlying his extraordinary success was his shrewd understanding of the financial possibilities of the extensive frontier expansion of that time. He built up an express shipping business between Albany and Utica, and used his profits to acquire land in Albany, Utica, Syracuse, and New York City.

By age 46 he was sufficiently wealthy to turn management of his commercial concerns over to others, focusing his time on real estate, money lending, and active citizenship. He achieved civic prominence, helping to organize the Chamber of Commerce and the Albany Savings Bank. In both cases he served as first vice-president with the last of the Dutch patroons, Stephen Van Rensselaer, serving as president.

These were the years of his son Henry's infancy. Henry's earliest memory was of the treaty marking the end of the War of 1812. This same year his father became a trustee in the Albany Academy and a director of the New York State Bank of Albany.

The early years of William of Albany's commercial progress were financially impressive and expansive. William, however, was widowed twice during this period. Three marriages within seven years, with the deaths of two wives, suggest a personal life which was not expansive but lonely and deeply unhappy. William of Albany first married in 1796 at age 24. Ten months later his wife died, eight days after giving birth to twins, both of whom survived to adulthood. A year and a half later he married again. This wife died after a year and ten months of marriage, leaving a daughter who lived to the age of 23.

Newspaper announcements indicate that William of Albany worked very hard during these years to achieve a public identity of control and mastery, in contrast to his private life. In May 1795, William opened a store with a partner. In December 1797 he opened a second store for receiving country produce. In November 1798 he announced the building of a tobacco factory. A fourth store was opened jointly with a second partner in 1800. This expansiveness suggests that William absorbed himself in a successful public career without facing the pain of his domestic life.

The following family anecdote indicates that his solid business identity was an alternative to the confusion and loss he felt about his marriages. It was said that shortly after his third marriage he encountered a woman coming up the stairs of his home. He rose from his work to meet her, announcing that Mrs. James was not in. This woman angrily reminded him that she indeed was his new wife.

William of Albany married his third wife, Catharine Barber, in 1803. He was 32 and she was 21. Catharine Barber James came from a distinguished and politically active family. She survived her husband by 27 years and played a strong and central role in the extended family. She gave birth to 10 children, 8 of whom survived to adulthood. Henry was the fourth of these. Catharine apparently found her own strong sense of identity as a matriarch in the extended family. She cared for the orphaned grandchildren in the family and maintained a household in which values other than those of her busy husband predominated in his absence.

William of Albany's business success provided a means of controlling his relationships with others and perhaps protected him from being preoccupied with the emotional stresses of his first two marriages. His identity was most secure when expressed in his work and his financial power. When he discovered that a business partner had cheated him, he grabbed him by his collar and literally dragged him to a judge.

"When old Billy James came to Syracuse," said a citizen who could remember his visits, "things went as *he* wished." (W. James 1920, I:3-4)

Something about William of Albany's formidable success, his indifference to family members, and the early death of the one son who did follow him into business, all counterbalanced by sufficient wealth, dissuaded the children from business careers. William of Albany survived and succeeded by maintaining a rigid and severe control over his investments. These investments did not include his family. He sought a similar control over his children, but they found escape from him in their domestic life.

The identity of an indulged child who was not required to earn a living predominated in the generation of William of Albany's children. Of all 11, only 2 pursued professions. These were Henry and his half-brother William. Both attended Princeton Theological Seminary, following the career their father was said to have rejected.

William was ordained in 1820, when Henry was eight years old. An eccentric but respected Presbyterian minister, he had an irregular and apparently troubled career. In 1835, after 15 years, he resigned from any direct ministerial duties and spent the remaining 33 years of his life studying philosophy and theology.

The ministry was crucial for these sons above and beyond the value of a career. Religion had a deeper significance than their father's rigid Calvinistic piety. There are suggestions of pain, loss, and identity confusion, followed by an intense striving for spiritual salvation, highly individualistic in form and directed toward a discovery of the true nature of one's relationship to God.

The similarities of temperament between the clergyman William and his half-brother Henry have been attributed by Perry (1935, vol. I) to the combined effects of Irish heredity and Calvinistic religious beliefs, energetic physique, and affluence and leisure. To these may be added early experiences of emotional distance from their father. Issues of identity became linked to special and frustrated expectations of sponsorship from William of Albany. Their careers expressed a competitive defiance against William of Albany's moral judgment and a search for spiritual support to replace the absence of a much-needed paternal presence.

In 1818 William of Albany retired from his business concerns. His son Robert was named by him to direct the business while he pursued commercial interests. Robert died in 1821, adding another loss to the family's experience.

William of Albany was made a trustee of the First Presbyterian Church in 1820. Shortly thereafter he became involved with Union College. The president of the college, Dr. Eliphalet Nott, had been his pastor at the First Presbyterian Church in Albany during the period of his second marriage some 20 years before.

In order to support the growth of Union College, Dr. Nott had entered into a legally and morally questionable agreement with the House of Yates and McIntyre. Nott and his lawyers Yates and McIntyre had convinced the state legislature to allow them to hold lotteries in order to finance the development of the college. The lawyers then entered into an agreement with Union to pay them more than $275,000, in exchange for which they were given responsibility for directing the lottery. In 1821 William advanced the college $56,000 to help cover expenses. The following year he loaned them an additional $33,354.

In 1822 William of Albany was the sole witness to a dual contract between Nott and Yates and McIntyre, in which Nott was secretly given a percentage of the profits for a President's Fund, whose use was unspecified. Speculation and massive debt led to confusion and potential financial ruin for both the firm and the college after the first lottery. William of Albany advanced $71,000 in exchange for a deed on the property of the college campus. When the lottery of 1825 failed, it led to further risks and speculation in relation to future lotteries. At this point William withdrew from active support of Dr. Nott's financial schemes. His loans were eventually repaid.

Meanwhile, William of Albany's financial situation had continued to improve. He was among the earliest promoters of the Erie Canal and achieved local status as a result. He delivered the oration at the celebration of its completion in 1825 in a practical and optimistic style. He commented:

> Nothing but the torpid stupidity of atheism can prevent the reflecting mind from perceiving the special intervention of providence in protecting and advancing our national honor and greatness. (Grattan 1932, 15-16)

William of Albany's faith was tempered by his trust in the stability of the material world. He willingly took financial risks and supported others who did so. Material success provided him with a means of reassurance and security, a sign of the special blessings of God on American capitalism. Financially he experienced a flexibility which his emotional and religious rigidity protected.

In the growing city of Albany, worldly status and success seemed the true vocation of man. Dr. Nott in his financial and entrepreneurial ventures turned to the world of finance as the method of spreading his version of God's message. He admired the worldly life and found the clergy at times unrealistic and overly protected. He felt more comfortable with confrontation and freely confided to doubting students that he had been spiritually troubled at one period in his life.

Unlike Dr. Nott's ambivalence about his career, William's sense of destiny as a businessman apparently never faltered. The tragedies of his life crystallized and reinforced his identity choice, and the world of the marketplace expressed for him a moral and spiritual assurance of God's blessing.

Like himself, the church was a pillar of the community. In its strength and success William of Albany could find a reflection and justification of the more secure aspects of his identity. Its morality demanded no emotional expression, as did the unhappy and disruptive early family years.

William of Albany in his dealings with Union College had transformed even his minister into a business partner over whom he exerted financial control. This triumph of economics allowed him to develop a relationship with Dr. Nott which was stable and reliable. William of Albany's financial resources stabilized and protected Dr. Nott's somewhat unstable and vulnerable character. He thus reinforced his own image of how the church should be, an institution whose growth and material development was a model of moral rigidity and sternness for the community.

Henry's Early Childhood

Henry James was born in 1811. His earliest memory was of having been taken outside by his nurse one evening to watch the celebration of the peace treaty signed with Great Britain in 1815. The event was a failure from Henry's point of view:

> That is, the only impression left by the illumination upon my imagination was the contrast of the awful dark of the sky with the feeble glitter of the streets; as if the animus of the display had been, not to eclipse the darkness, but to make it visible. You of course may put what interpretation you choose upon the incident, but it seems to me rather emblematic of the intellect, that its earliest sensible foundation should thus be laid in "a horror of great darkness." (W. James 1884, 145-46)

This memory reveals a crucial issue for Henry. The world of the senses, he suggests, begins with a horror of great darkness, a horror which arises out of a flash of illumination. Henry's view of his father paralleled this experience. He struggled to maintain an idealized, imaginative belief in his father's loving attention, but frequently he found himself in an angry intellectual struggle against the kinds of relationships which his father actually developed. Although he would cling to the belief that his father was a deeply caring person, he was constantly confronted by other images of paternal sponsorship in which his father was hostile and demanding. Henry's intellectual constructions focused on the bright, affectionate side of his relationship with his father rather than its potential darkness of moral condemnation. The celebration of peace which the memory notes suggested a hope for some future time in which such light would not be a failure.

Henry's next comments directly concern his father:

> When I was very young I do not remember to have had much intellectual contact with my father save at family prayers and at meals, for he was always occupied during the day with business; and even in the frank domestic intercourse of the evening, when he was fond of hearing his children read to him, and would frequently exercise them in their studies, I cannot recollect that he ever questioned me about my out-of-door occupations, or about my companions, or showed any extreme solicitude about my standing in school. (W. James 1884, 146–47)

Henry experienced an absence of paternal influence in his life. His father did not seem to recognize his capacity for creative and imaginative play and thought nor did he seem to be particularly concerned about the more formal components of learning. Thus the freedom Henry experienced was insufficient evidence of paternal interest. His intellect was ignored; it was left to develop in darkness.

He continues:

> He was certainly a very easy parent, and I might have been left to regard him perhaps as a rather indifferent one, if it had not been for a severe illness . . . which confined me for a long time to the house, when his tenderness to me showed itself so assiduous and indeed extreme as to give me an exalted sense of his affection. My wound had been very severe, being followed by a morbid process in the bone which ever and anon called for some sharp surgery; and on these occasions I remember—for the use of anaesthetics was still wholly undrempt of—his sympathy with my sufferings was so excessive that my mother had the greatest possible difficulty in imposing due prudence upon his expression of it. (W. James 1884, 147)

Henry was an active child who found great joy in the outdoors, until he was severely injured in a fire at the age of 13. A student at the Albany Academy, of which his father was a trustee, Henry had been playing tow-ball in the park. The following description of the incident comes from a fellow student:

> On a summer afternoon, the older students would meet Professor Henry in the Park, in front of the Academy, where amusement and instruction would be given in balloon-flying, the motive power being heated air supplied from a tow ball saturated with spirits of turpentine. When one of these air-ships took fire, the ball would be dropt for the boys, when it was kicked here and there, a roll of fire. [One day when] young James had a sprinkling of this [turpentine] on his pantaloons, one of these balls was sent into the open windows of Mrs. Gilchrist's stable. [James] thinking only of conflagration, rushed to the hayloft and stamped out the flame, but burned his leg. (W. James 1920, I:7–8)

For two years Henry remained in bed, undergoing two operations. His right leg was amputated twice, once below and once above the knee.

Henry's amputation had a tremendous influence on his image of his father; William of Albany began to appear over-solicitous rather than indifferent toward his son. Because of his accident, Henry was able to feel cared for by his father, whose brief attention to Henry's amputation contrasted to his disinterest in the other dimensions of his son's life. For Henry, the experience was like a blinding light. For the first time he experienced what he had wanted and missed from his father. The development of their relationship became an experience both of darkness and confusion and of inspiring, if terrifying, light.

Although the intervention of Henry's mother set limits on their intensity, his feelings toward his father underwent a radical change. He developed an exalted sense of his father's affection, a psychological gain which counteracted the loss of his leg. The unreality and excessiveness of these feelings paralleled the emotional turmoil of his physical injury. In this idealization, actual memory seems to have been put in the service of emotional need. From this time on Henry regarded his father's distance as the product of excessive sensitivity. It is difficult to accept this view of William of Albany without question. Henry's experience links a crucial idealizing fantasy with the conceivable possibility that his father, responding to other losses in his life, made a brief and uncharacteristic special effort to foster his son's survival. However, the memory exists only in Henry's reports.

Henry's sudden moment of illumination both heightened and threatened his sense of being cared for. Maternal figures offered more continuous and less dramatic relationships. His mother was "a good wife and mother, nothing else, — save, to be sure a kindly friend and neighbor" (W. James 1884, 147). Henry's closeness to her was enhanced following his injury. It was less intense, however:

> My mother, I repeat, was maternity itself in form; and I remember, as a touching evidence of this, that I have frequently seen her during my protracted illness, when I had been greatly reduced and required the most watchful nursing, come to my bedside fast asleep with her candle in her hand, and go through the forms of covering my shoulders, adjusting my pillows, and so forth, just as carefully as if she were awake. (W. James 1884, 148)

In his mother's response Henry saw the reaction of a sleepwalker, solicitous but unconsciously so. Her care-taking lost some of its meaning for him because she accepted it as a part of her self-effacing maternal identity. It was not a recognition of his separate needs but an enactment of a role. Perhaps this left him more comfortable but apparently he remained wide awake in the middle of the night with no one to talk to about what he was feeling.

Henry in fact found little comfort in family life as a child. He experienced "a certain lack of oxygen . . . which I may characterize as the lack of any ideal but that of self-preservation" (W. James 1884, 152). This atmosphere developed under the influence of the religious beliefs held by his father and sanctioned by the clergymen who frequently visited his home.

Henry's family life was ruled by these ministers, who were the successful competitors for his father's attention and values. The pious orientation which was taught by the church undermined the joy and spontaneity of his childhood. Only on Christmas were the children allowed their innocent fun. Sundays in particular were stifling:

> That is, we were taught not to play, not to dance, nor to sing, not to read storybooks, not to con over our school-lessons for Monday even, not to whistle, not to ride the pony, nor to take a walk in the country, nor a swim in the river; nor, in short, to do anything which nature specially craved. . . . Nothing is so hard for a child as *not-to-do*; that is, to keep his hands and feet and tongue in enforced inactivity. It is a cruel wrong to put such an obligation upon him, while his reflective faculties are still undeveloped, and his senses urge him to unrestricted action. (W. James 1884, 154–55)

The church's masculine, paternal, restrictive values symbolized and supported his father's moral demands and his emotional distance. His father, who seemed to have so little time and interest for him, welcomed into his company clergymen who embodied a rigid, restrictive morality. Henry was excluded from this by the childhood enthusiasms which contrasted with adult accomplishment and self-interest. This problem emerged in the list of "not-to's" by which he felt oppressed as a child. The restrictive, pious attitude of his father stimulated the child's fear and rebellion. As an adult, Henry continued to resent the self-righteousness of conventional church-goers. His critique of the traditional church was based in part on his continuing reluctance to deny the spontaneity which he remembered as so important, and so unsupported, during his childhood.

As he grew, Henry's conflicts about control became private struggles with the God in whom he was taught to believe, a prohibitive paternal figure capable of condemning him for his jealous competition with the clergy. The doctrine of original sin was especially terrifying to him. He describes it as a "puerile and disgusting caricature of the gospel . . . dogmatic fouling of the creative name" (W. James 1884, 158–59). He denies ever having believed this doctrine in his heart; rather, he passively endured what was imposed on him. His teachers led him to adopt the belief that "a chronic apathy existed on God's part towards me, superinduced by Christ's work upon the active enmity he had formerly felt toward us" (W. James 1884, 160).

Henry converted this image of God's apathy into one of personal hostility, leading to attempts to communicate by "the most profuse acknowledgments of indebtedness, and the most profuse promises of future payment" (W. James 1884, 161). Because of his youth he could not evaluate the truth or falsity of the religious dogma. He accepted it solely on the basis of the church's authority.

Henry escaped these terrors by secretly testing his father's generosity. When he was seven or eight, he and his friends began to frequent a confectioner's shop where Henry occasionally built up a debt of as much as 20¢. He learned that he could pay for his candy by secretly taking money from a drawer in his father's dressing table. His knowledge of his "father's magical drawer" produced in him a "timorous sigh of relief" and was his introduction to the "tree of knowledge of good and evil" (W. James 1884, 166). Moral development had become something more complicated than defiance or obedience. It involved his capacity to imagine a good father and his willingness to risk acting on that image.

Henry praises his father for his sensitivity to his children's needs. That sensitivity, however, appears to be the imaginary product of a theft and a fantasy rather than an actual experience.

The intense suffering which Henry was forced to undergo led him to idealize his father as a means of preserving his sense of himself. Freud noted the presence of deep ambivalence in a son's earliest idealization of his father and attributed the intensity of the idealization to the son's fantasy of possible castration by his father. Henry's idealization intensified at the time of his injury. However it was not a reaction to a fantasy or a verbal threat of injury but to a real and painful danger in his life. Therefore the positive idealization did not gradually establish itself as does the typical young boy's in the reassuring protectiveness of a father who accepts his son's growing identification. Instead it temporarily unified the anger and terror with an overpowering wish to survive.

Henry enlisted his idealization of his father in this process following a short-lived experience of intense involvement on the part of William of Albany. The brief closeness left Henry to cope with a second loss, that of his father's concern. The capacity to idealize had been distorted in Henry's life by becoming part of a larger and more intense struggle to survive, undertaken essentially alone.

As he began to recover, Henry resumed his studies at home with Joseph Henry, who had become a professor of mathematics at the Albany Academy in 1826. They remained close friends for many years. Joseph Henry later pursued a distinguished career in science, teaching at Princeton and eventually becoming director of the Smithsonian Institution. By assuming responsibility for Henry's education and sharing with the boy his love of science, he helped to fill the place left empty by Henry's father.

In 1828, three years after his accident, Henry had recovered sufficiently to enter the junior class at nearby Union College. (Much later in his life he wrote in a letter to one of his sons that he had left home with a serious drinking problem, which he had acquired during his years of illness. Nothing is known about when and how he overcame the problem, or its influence on his early adulthood.) Henry lived with his father's friend, Dr. Nott, the college president. The college still owed William of Albany money and therefore required his continuing support. This was a period of some anxiety on the part of John Yates as to the overall intentions of William of Albany. That September he wrote to Dr. Nott:

> We are now, as it were, situated on a MAGAZINE OF POWDER, with the torch in the hand of a man who is our friend today, but we know not how long, and he can blow us up when he pleases. (Hislop 1971, 304)

William of Albany had been made a Union College trustee the year before and it seems that Yates greatly exaggerated the threat he posed the college. However, James was putting financial pressure on Yates and McIntyre, having refused to renew notes on debts they owed to him.

The influence of college on Henry was complex. The institution itself was marked by a sentiment of optimism and expansiveness. Although Union like other colleges required strict attendance of classes, church, and prayers, Dr. Nott in his customary openness allowed the first fraternities in America to be formed on campus. For Henry the opportunity to develop special friendships was a significant experience, unavailable to him during his earlier confinement. When it was decided among the fraternity brothers that they should wear badges, Henry went to Albany to obtain them, probably becoming the first American to wear a fraternity pin.

Dr. Nott has been described as an instructor who encouraged his students to develop independent opinions. His classes were taught in a spirit of tolerance and self-expression. Consequently his students pursued a variety of theological orientations in their later lives. The more intensely religious found him to be lukewarm and lax and his true strengths seem to have been in the areas of pragmatic action and insightful questioning. His openness may well have reflected an underlying ambivalence about the ministry and a frustrated desire to be more involved in the business world, with its high risks and possibilities of wealth and personal power. He frequently undertook business ventures but was never particularly successful. Consequently he remained in his role as a minister and a college president, interpreting this role rather liberally in regard to financial speculation and development.

Dr. Nott's influence on Henry can only be a matter of conjecture. Henry entered college without having attended school during his earlier teenage years. His experience of relationships was limited therefore to his family. He quickly involved himself in a special organization and was anxious to display its insignia to the world, indicating perhaps a continuing need for close and special relationships.

Guidance, however, was hard for Henry to come by at Union College. Neither his fraternity brothers nor Dr. Nott seem to have intervened in Henry's abuse of his father's funds: "his practise of giving in payment for the luxuries which he relished—good cigars, oysters, smart tailoring, books—drafts upon the credit of his opulent sire" (Warren 1934, 16).

Henry's behavior was like that of the prodigal son. Apparently he needed to throw away an inheritance and to challenge the authority of his father in order to establish his own identity. For a boy whose freedom had been crucial and who had lost his physical capacity to run, Union College promised liberty. He was no longer exposed to his father's moralistic temperament, having become dependent on a view of William of Albany which idealized his generosity. When his image of his father lost its familial context, he felt free enough to test the restrictions of family life. He believed they reflected the influence of the rigid clergy rather than his father's true feelings. This restriction disappeared in the home of the liberal Dr. Nott and in a college which his father was helping to finance.

Henry began to challenge his boundaries, drawing on a purely monetary view of his father's achievements and at the same time demanding his father's indulgence. His actions suggest a naive hope that his quite wealthy father would pay for whatever he wanted and realize that the true test of their relationship was in his ability to give to his son.

Henry became the intemperate consumer of the "segars" which his father had made his first profits manufacturing and selling. He mocked his father in this way, showing that his father's success had not liberalized his values and identity. William of Albany still held rather tightly onto the household purse strings despite his financial flexibility. He was unwilling to make an investment in his son despite the thousands of dollars he had entrusted to Dr. Nott. This focused the issue of William of Albany's emotional rigidity.

It is impossible to know whether a dialogue between father and son took place over several months, or whether William of Albany was suddenly shocked to learn that his son had been drawing on his credit. Henry however demanded too much and received a sound scolding from the distinguished lawyer Archibald McIntyre, of Yates and McIntyre. The letter is dated November 12, 1829, which was during Henry's second year at college. It reads, in part:

> I have heard, and your friends generally have heard enough of your conduct to cause us much pain and solicitude for your safety and future usefulness. I consider you on the very verge of ruin. . . . Allow me then to entreat that you will for the future repose

yourself upon your father and mother, and take their advice in everything. Indulge in no expenses whatever that shall not be known to and approved by them. . . . Let your studies too as far as possible be comfortable to your father's wishes. You intimated to me that you disliked the law. . . . On speaking to your father on this head, however, I found him inflexibly fixed on your studying the law, or at all events on studying one of the learned professions. . . . Some consider you already lost, irretrievably lost. I am not, however, one of those. I cannot believe that a young man of good parts, with wealth to support him in well doing (but with none without performing his duty), with numerous and anxious friends, can be such an idiot as to throw away all these advantages, and become a loathing to himself and his best friends. (Warren 1934, 17)

The tone of the letter is severe and it certainly is noteworthy that William of Albany chose not to write it himself but to have McIntyre do so. Ironically and perhaps hypocritically, this friend, who had gambled with and lost hundreds of thousands of dollars in the lottery, was shocked at Henry's expenditures. Henry is imitating the behavior of these legal friends of his father without having paid his dues.

Perhaps William of Albany had hoped that Henry might enter the firm of Yates and McIntyre, preserving the shaky relationship which existed among William of Albany, Nott, and Yates and McIntyre. So long as Henry was a student at Union he preserved the safety of the college from exposure at William of Albany's hands and from scandal and possible financial ruin for the lawyers handling the lottery. Henry's presence in the Nott household was an issue of more than moral consequence for McIntyre.

Law would have been a very practical career choice for Henry, for the financial investments of his father involved frequent legal knowledge and procedures. But above and beyond this William wished his children to do something useful with themselves.

William of Albany relied on his wife and friends to raise his son, then rigidly insisted on deciding his career in a way which would enhance his business security. This contrasts with the image Henry presents of his father as too emotionally invested to be sufficiently paternal and stern. When confronted with this contradictory and confusing reality, Henry fled to Boston.

Henry James, Jr., later recalled a visit to Boston with his father in which the latter had referred to this flight as a result of

a misunderstanding, if indeed not a sharp rupture, for the time, with a highly generous but also on occasion strongly protesting parent at Albany, a parent displeased with the course he had taken or had declined to take (there was a tradition among us that he had been for a period quite definitely "wild"), and relief from further discussion with whom he had sought and had more or less found, on that spot. ([1913] 1956, 349)

Henry's relief might be characterized as relief from the contrast between his idealized image of his father and William of Albany's actual demandingness. The contrast was terrifying. It threatened the sense of protection and caring which he secretly accepted as his father's true feeling toward him.

Henry left for Boston less than a month after receiving the letter from McIntyre. This could not have been an easy trip for a young man with one leg as there was no railroad at that time from Albany to Boston.

William of Albany found his son's flight scandalous. To McIntyre he wrote:

> [Henry] has so debased himself as to leave his parents houses in the character of a swindler, etc. etc. — details presented today — are the order which I enclose as a specimen of his progress in arts of low vileness — and unblushing falsehood; — such will be practiced in N.Y. — in book stores — Taylors etc. — and in the same as dfts on me etc.; — all of which will meet him direct — and lodge him in a prison of some kind directly; a fellow from Schenectady was after him today for 50 to 60 drs — [in a note I understand] for segars and oysters. . . . Townsend — Sons — and others from the College have reported through the City — that he is gone to Boston — and I understand he told the man who gave the cloth that he was going there — but deception is of no consequence in his case — they will find him and he will find his reward, poor being. (Warren 1934, 18)

William of Albany hardly seems in a state of mind to protect or defend his son. He apparently had not covered Henry's debts and expected that he would go to prison.

Henry's creditors did not seek him out, however, and he settled into a comfortable life in Boston. To a friend and tutor at Union he wrote: "After all the great step has been taken . . . and I am alone in my pilgrimage" (Warren 1934, 18). He read proof and translated for the office of Jenks and Palmer. He lived with the Jenks family and found Mr. Jenks scholarly and encouraging and Mrs. Jenks an accomplished lady. They introduced Henry to the best society, and his capacity to work was stimulated:

> I now go on with the study of languages much more thoroughly than I should have found it necessary had I remained at home. It is indispensable that I should. My ambition is awakened; I have here every advantage and the least shall not be slighted. (Warren 1934, 19)

Henry found the encouragement he needed from Mr. Jenks. This provided him with the support his father had refused to give without forcing a confrontation between father and son. In this accepting environment he apparently repented his earlier wildness. He returned to Union College, graduating in 1830. His father was invited to sit in on the college faculty meeting which passed Henry and his classmates for their degrees.

For a period Henry reconciled himself with his father's wishes. He studied Blackstone as a senior. According to family legend he continued to study law more seriously following graduation and undertook a few business ventures. He also maintained some independence, for he worked for five months as an editor of the Albany *Daily Craftsman*, a publication issued in opposition to an Albany newspaper.

The Financial and Spiritual Inheritance

William of Albany died in 1832. His obituary in the *Daily Albany Arbus* stated, in part:

> He was identified with the growth and prosperity of our city. Everywhere we see his footsteps. Turn where we may, and there are the results of his informing mind — his energy — and his vast wealth. His plans of improvement embraced the entire city; and there is scarcely a street or square which does not exhibit some mark of his improving hand, or some proof of his opulence. (Grattan 1932, 20)

His final tribute to the importance of financial stability and hard work, however, was his will.

Although he provided all his children and grandchildren with "an annuity for life . . . as shall be sufficient to supply the probable actual wants of such individuals" (Grattan 1932, 19), the $3 million fortune which William of Albany had accumulated was otherwise to be distributed only to those who did not lead "a grossly immoral, idle or dishonorable life" (Grattan 1932, 19). Examples were made of William and Henry who were punished for their theological orientation by being cut off with only a small annuity. In his will William of Albany explained:

> In pursuance of these designs (to provide sufficient support and education for those under age) and in view of the lamentable consequences which so frequently result to young persons brought up in affluence from coming at once into the possession of property, I have also determined that this trust shall continue, and that the final division of my estate shall not take place until the youngest of my children and grand-children living at the date of this my will and attaining the age of twenty-one years shall have attained that age. And in order moreover to provide against accidental irregularities and diversities of my condition which at the expiration of the trust may exist among *cestuy que* trusts, but more especially with a view to discourage prodigality and vice and furnish an incentive to economy and usefulness, I have further determined to invest my trustees with extensive discretionary powers in regard to the disposition of my property. (Grattan 1932, 18)

William wished to use his wealth as a stabilizing and moralizing force, a means of "punishing idleness and vice and rewarding virtue" (Grattan 1932, 19). In the face of limited family relations this rigidity stood out not as guidance but as unnecessary restriction. William's great grandson reported:

> Indeed, there appears to have been only one matter in which he was rigorous with his family: his Presbyterianism was of the stiffest kind, and in his old age he sacrificed even his affections for what he considered the true faith. (W. James 1920, I:4)

William's will was sufficiently strict regarding his wife's estate and that of his children to cause them to take it to court and have it broken. This was enacted on December 30, 1836. Henry received a large parcel of real estate which yielded about $10,000 annually, freeing him from ever having to earn his living.

In the interim period between his father's death and the breaking of the will Henry experienced an intensification of his religious concerns. He was again confronted with his father's sternness and his refusal to provide emotional support. His religious needs increased in response to this disappointment. His search for paternal and spiritual protection led him back to his former tutor. Joseph Henry had left Albany to teach at Princeton in 1832. In 1835 Henry joined him there as a student in the theological seminary. In the same year his half-brother William, who had graduated from this seminary, terminated his activities as a minister and applied himself to theological research.

Henry's excursion into the professional ministry lasted for two academic years. Later in life he presented himself as having almost naively approached that profession only to be angered and disappointed at its dogmatic, institutionalized, professional orientation. He

> never knew a misgiving as to the perfect truth of its dogmas, until I had begun to prepare myself for its professional ministry. Then I could no longer evade the enormous difficulties which inhered in its philosophy. . . . I was sure that while orthodoxy had somehow succeeded to a celestial inheritance, it was yet a most unrighteous steward of that inheritance; but how to dispossess it God alone knew. (Grattan 1932, 29)

The clergy had been a target for his anger with his father in his childhood and now again showed an intolerable rigidity. He had turned to the ministry as a source of support, but God had an "unrighteous steward" who delivered his message of sin and salvation to the world. Dr. Nott's liberal values had not permeated Princeton. One faculty member, Dr. Charles Hodge, "once boasted that he had taught theology 50 years without ever introducing a new idea" (Warren 1934, 22).

Following what was becoming a pattern of flight, Henry requested a six-month's leave of absence from Princeton to go to England. He did not realize at that time that he would never return to the seminary, or perhaps he had learned that it was best not to burn his bridges behind him.

Henry had left school by early May 1837. This was less than four months after he had received his inheritance through the court's decision about his father's will. In September he departed for Europe, having been invited by his friend Joseph Henry to join him in Paris. Henry chose first to visit his father's family in Ireland where he presented an image of a wealthy young man. Later he joined Joseph Henry and they traveled together. He visited the famous scientist Michael Faraday for whom Joseph had given Henry a letter of introduction. Faraday in turn introduced Henry to the theology of Robert Sandeman.

Sandeman, who had died in the year that William of Albany was born (1771), became a spiritual and philosophical father to Henry's theology. Sandeman, like Henry, had rebelled against the traditional Calvinism of his day, augmenting the Glasite movement of his father-in-law with a somewhat more fanatical religious philosophy. Sandeman's theology focused on faith rather than on moral behavior and was critical toward the traditional clergy.

Young (1951) points out that Sandeman justified his orientation toward faith through his doctrine of the saving influence of the life of Christ. It was only a matter of a shift in focus for Henry to place emphasis on the faith of the believer rather than on the object of that faith. William of Albany's financial decisions paralleled this change. He moved from the more traditional orientation of the Dutch patroons and their passive form of real estate economy to the active development of the western territories and the Erie Canal. Henry's theories moved the believer into a similar dynamic developmental relationship with his material. What his father could do with land and money, Henry could do with faith.

Henry protected his idealized view of his father, heavenly and earthly, by a focus on the conceptual process of mastery and activity. This was a form of identifying with his father's financial style, which William of Albany developed at a time when he was coping with his own significant personal losses. Theology was the material which Henry transformed. This was different from that of his father and yet the process was in many ways parallel to William of Albany's successful business life.

One might say that Henry developed a foundation and a justification for the image of the close experience whose apparent disappearance caused so much pain. Henry developed an image of an unspoken and unacknowledged permissiveness and closeness with his father. This could not be expressed directly because William of Albany was unable to apply his financial dynamism to the world of emotion and theology. Henry was driven to do so, becoming perhaps the clergyman of his father's unacknowledged dreams, the man who could expand himself using theology with the freedom of a financial genius. Henry however maintained a theoretical rigidity. His idealism matched his father's materialism in its singular significance. Neither could move beyond the realm in which he found himself in control of his expectations.

Henry remained in England for about one year. When he returned he prepared a copy of Sandeman's *Letters on Theron and Aspasio* (1838), writing the preface himself and defending the author against the reproach of traditional theologians. He followed this with a privately published pamphlet, *Remarks on the Apostolic Gospel* (1840), copies of which unfortunately have not survived.

Henry's exposure to Sandeman had supported his interest in theological speculation as a way of resolving his feelings about his father. On returning to America he found that the predominant interest of the intellectual community was not religion but social experience. The spiritual dimension of American progressive life was being articulated most fully by Emerson. It was a spirit of optimism and tranquility, in marked contrast to the pain and doubt that Henry had been experiencing.

In 1842 Henry went to one of Emerson's lectures. The image of natural purity that Emerson projected fascinated him. He immediately wrote to Emerson, suggesting that they meet. He told Emerson that he believed him to be a man who "in very truth was seeking the realities of things" (Perry 1935, I:39).

Henry was most impressed by Emerson's sense of truth, which echoed a positive dimension of William of Albany's spiritual rigidity, his insistence on the absolute truth of Presbyterianism. Henry, however, misrepresented himself as sharing this interest. In fact he sought not objective truth but belief. He looked to relationships for intense psychological encounters rather than stable and secure understanding.

> This is in substance what I said to myself. Now that I have told it to you also, you have become a sort of confidant between me and myself, and so in a manner bound to promote harmony there. If you shrink from the confidence thus thrust upon you, I shall certainly be blamed by *myself*, for making so indiscreet a communication to you; but if you abide it, *I* shall with equal certainty be highly felicitated by *myself* for achieving a result so undeniably inauspicious to both. (Perry 1935, I:40–41)

For Henry, Emerson was more than a fellow seeker. He provided Henry with the experience of an idealized closeness with a father figure. This raised Henry's hopes that he had finally found the intimacy he had been seeking. This intimacy, however, threatened Henry, for it stimulated the terror of disappointment which had permeated his interactions with his father. He needed to pull back from his wish for intimacy and examine it introspectively. He had to test his love.

In his next letter Henry wrote to the "Invisible Emerson, the Emerson that thinks and feels and lives" (Perry 1935, I:41). This was the idealized Emerson who was invisible because he lived only in Henry's expectations. The invisible Emerson was the object of his attention, not

> the Emerson that talks and bewitches one out of his serious thought when one talks to him, by the beautiful serenity of his behavior. This latter Emerson I shall begin to hate soon for keeping my stupid eyes so continually away from the profounder Emerson who alone can do one any good. (Perry 1935, I:41)

Henry was soothed by Emerson's example, but he also was frustrated because he was unable to accept Emerson with the serenity with which Emerson accepted him. He wanted to understand Emerson, but he feared that closeness could cause him to forget what he needed.

Henry's expectations could not be met by Emerson, who was more passive than Henry in his sense of faith. Emerson felt no pressing need to search for what he required. Rather he sought to articulate an image of optimism and goodness as a means of perpetuating a sense of calm and security. Henry feared that Emerson could not be trusted with his emotional needs because he seemed to feel so little pain himself. He appeared to have no experience of wanting, no sense of self. After some reflection Henry could not accept this: "I know you have the same wants as I have, deep down in your bosom hidden from my sight, and it is by these I want somewhat to know you" (Perry 1935, I:42). Perhaps Henry had also wanted to know his father in this way.

Since Emerson's personal example could not help Henry, he turned to science, with its laws, facts, and underlying sense of order. He was torn between the control implied by idealistic faith and that of scientific ideas. The security of science was symbolized by the reassurance of Joseph Henry's more limited but more trustworthy support in his childhood, in contrast to Henry's idealistic image of his father.

Henry corresponded at this time with Joseph Henry, who had stopped to visit him on a trip to New York but had missed him. Henry regretted this particularly in the light of his renewed wish to come to some understanding about science. He wrote Joseph a letter expressing his frustration at being unable to find a single book that would present the underlying spiritual principles of science. Joseph's reply to Henry indicated that his questions were similar to those of his scientific contemporaries:

> The tendency of science is to higher and higher, or rather I should say wider and wider, generalizations, and could we be possessed of sufficient intelligence we would probably see all the phenomena of the external universe, and perhaps all those of the spiritual, reduced to the operation of a single and simple law of *Divine* will. . . . Our elementary

books are entirely destitute of the true scientific spirit, and generally inculcate the idea that science consists in a mere accumulation and arrangement of facts. (Perry 1935, I:19)

Henry received more support from Joseph Henry than from Emerson in his attempt to define a philosophy which would link the Creator, science, and human experience. One senses that Joseph Henry articulated his search for a sponsoring experience in science more concretely than Emerson expressed his inherent sense of philosophical congruence. Neither of these two men felt as disenchanted with his profession as did Henry, however. He sensed that he could not trust either the scientific or the philosophic currents of American thought. Needing both the ideal and the experiential, he sought some means of integrating the two.

Having found little in the way of support in America for his intellectual preoccupations, Henry decided in 1843 to return to Europe. He had married in 1840, and was accompanied on this trip by his wife, his sister-in-law, and his two infant sons.

It seems quite likely that Henry sought replacements for Emerson in Europe as he searched for a more confrontative style of relationship. He asked for and received from Emerson a letter of introduction to Carlyle. Henry had described Carlyle to Emerson as "the very best interpreter of a spiritual philosophy that could be devised for *this age*" (Warren 1934, 41).

The encounter Henry had with Carlyle was very disturbing. He apparently sensed, even at the beginning of their relationship, that Carlyle's particular form of Calvinistic thought had merely noted and cynically commented upon emotional suffering and evil without bringing these problems to any particular resolution. Carlyle had sensed the separation between the ideal and the experiential aspects of relationships but had resolved this by cultivating a negative and pitying attitude toward others. Many years later Henry began an article for the *Atlantic* entitled "Some Personal Recollections of Carlyle" as follows:

> Thomas Carlyle is incontestably dead at last, by the acknowledgement of all newspapers. I had, however, the pleasure of an intimate intercourse with him when he was an infinitely deader man than he is now, or ever will be again, I am persuaded, in the remotest *seculum seculorum*. I undoubtedly felt myself at the time every whit as dead (spiritually) as he was; and, to tell the truth, I never found him adverse to admit my right of insight in regard to myself. But I could never bring him, much as he continually inspired me so to do, to face the philosophic possibility of this proposition in regard to himself. (H. James 1881, 593)

Henry used his wit and sophistication to characterize his disappointment with Carlyle. His imagery suggests that his sense of inner deadness was increased by Carlyle's cynicism. The relationship enhanced the fear and isolation Henry felt by "maintaining every popular illusion" (H. James 1881, 593) that truth was valuable only for its esthetic and intellectual function and had no relation to a person's search for meaning. Carlyle was entirely fixated on his own genius and unable to use it "to help a struggling brother on to daylight" (H. James 1881, 602).

Henry could not accept a concept of evil intentions toward others. His impressions of Carlyle were influenced by Carlyle's orientation toward evil in men. It stimulated his hidden fear that relationships were destructive, and that idealized figures might choose to impose pain rather than alleviate it.

> Carlyle had very much of the narrowness, intellectual and moral, which one might expect to find in a descendant of the old Covenanting stock, bred to believe in God as essentially inhuman, and in man, accordingly, as exposed to a great deal of divine treachery and vindictiveness, which were liable to come rattling about his devoted ears the moment his back was turned. (H. James 1881, 595)

Carlyle was able to feel admiration and pity for other men but never genuine identification with their suffering. He viewed "the good and evil in our nature as final or absolute quantities, and saw no way, consequently, of ever utilizing the evil element" (H. James 1881, 601). Henry found him "fixed . . . in so intense and irritable a literary *self*-consciousness" (H. James 1881, 602). Carlyle had developed an idealized view of himself to replace his disappointed idealizations of others.

While Emerson had stimulated a positive but empty image of William of Albany, Carlyle stimulated a negative and damning image of him. Perhaps Henry's father had seen the depth of his suffering but had responded with emotional indifference or even cynical pleasure at seeing someone else in pain. If evil were something out of man's control, then one could do no more than accept it in oneself and hope to be spared from too much of it. This formulation would explain William of Albany's indifference to Henry's suffering but would disintegrate the notion that his father had understood and had genuinely reached out to him.

Retreating from his disappointment with Carlyle, Henry went to Windsor to pursue his writing. He recounts his experience there:

> In the spring of 1844 I was living with my family in the neighborhood of Windsor, England, much absorbed in the study of the Scriptures. Two or three years before I had made an important discovery, as I fancied; namely, that the book of Genesis was not intended to throw a direct light upon our natural or race history, but was an altogether mystical or *spiritual* creation and providence. (W. James 1884, 58)

Henry felt extremely ambivalent about the direction in which his thought had taken him. He could construct an ideal, stabilizing image of relationships, but he found his actual experience was one of disruption and disappointment. He became increasingly introspective. He began to believe that his philosophical interests were freeing him from a rigid physicalistic concept of creation. At the same time his interpretive work was leading him to view the Bible as a philosophical introduction to faith rather than a literal description of history. His lectures in New York had convinced him that his ideas were valuable but required further development.

Henry had left the confinement of America. He felt free and confident. Yet the doubts that had emerged in his letters again surfaced, this time not in the form of disappointment in his friends but in a more personal way:

> One day, however, towards the close of May, having eaten a comfortable dinner, I remained sitting at the table after the family had dispersed, idly gazing at the embers in the grate, thinking of nothing, and feeling only the exhilaration incident to a good digestion, when suddenly—in a lightening-flash as it were—"fear came upon me, and trembling, which made all my bones to shake." To all appearance it was a perfectly insane and abject terror, without ostensible cause, and only to be accounted for, to my perplexed imagination, by some damned shape squatting invisible to me within the precincts of the room, and raying out from his fetid personality influences fatal to life. (W. James 1884, 59)

Henry, sitting alone, presumably confident and well cared for, was confronted by a squatting, stinking, invisible figure. The devil presented himself to Henry in a manner which displayed evil communication and an accompanying threat of death.

In Henry's fantasy evil was externalized. This represented an emerging awareness of some truth in Carlyle's moral philosophy. Carlyle acknowledged suffering, which Henry was afraid to do. Having accepted it, Carlyle used his sense of moral superiority to justify a rigid view of himself. For Carlyle, identity was a matter of stoic acceptance of one's lot in life. This represented a step backward from Emerson's sense of his own social and personal responsibility, although Emerson had minimized self-consciousness in the process.

While Emerson had idealized humanity, Carlyle had done so with the self. Emerson had provided an unrealistic and untrustworthy escape for Henry from his father's rigidity. Carlyle forced an overwhelming and inescapable confrontation with it. In response Henry sank into a deep depression. Evil became such a potent concept that it seemed to emanate from the world. The fresh air Henry longed for became fetid. It stank of spiritual death. Without a more flexible image of relationships, Henry could not assert a sense of his own identity.

Henry's first response was terror and a driving desire to run:

> The thing had not lasted ten seconds before I felt myself a wreck; that is, reduced from a state of firm, vigorous, joyful manhood to one of almost helpless infancy. The only self-

control I was capable of exerting was to keep my seat. I felt the greatest desire to run incontinently to the foot of the stairs and shout for help to my wife,—to run to the roadside even, and appeal to the public to protect me; but by an immense effort I controlled these frenzied impulses, and determined not to budge from my chair till I had recovered my lost self-possession. (W. James 1881, 59-60)

This passage reflects not only current anxieties but echoes of childhood stresses. The "wreck" suggests the cripple reduced from his freedom to a state of dependency. Running could no longer liberate him. "The only self-control I was capable of exerting was to keep my seat." His spiritual state paralleled his childhood accident.

Henry's development reflected a theme of running from interpersonal crises, with his father, with Emerson, with Carlyle. In this way he had maintained a belief in his own ideological freedom. When relationships disappointed him he could re-establish his identity and sense of mastery by distancing himself from them. Yet the freedom involved denial of his need for others, a problem that threatened to undermine the sense of identity which he experienced.

Henry expressed the childhood complaint, the hate and resentment he felt toward his loss and confinement, and the emptiness of being alone in his pain. Self-control, once found through activity, now demanded that he keep his seat. The evil figure was squatting, thus mocking Henry's required posture and his passive isolation.

Henry's image of his father's caring presence became, in his moment of despair, an image of death. His father was symbolized as an evil, damaging, dangerous figure who intended to hurt him. In reaction to this horrifying possibility, Henry's loneliness could emerge in a more genuine manner. He became depressed. He faced the emptiness that was inside of him.

Henry then began to integrate the pain he felt into his sense of identity. The process continued for about two years, during which he slowly began to experience periods of relief. He noted "a most important change operating in my will and understanding" (W. James 1881, 62) in that he began to seek truth through some form other than his previous ideas. Following the ideas of Emanuel Swedenborg, he began to attribute his terror to a false sense of self. He found salvation in his growing acceptance of relationships, particularly with his family. During this time he formulated his unique religious philosophy.

Marriage and Early Family Years

Henry married Mary Walsh on July 28, 1840. Mary was the sister of a former fellow student of Henry's at Princeton Theological Seminary. Both had left the seminary before graduation, sharing dissatisfaction with its traditional Presbyterian theology.

Henry's ambivalence about close relationships with men was complemented by a rigidity in his relationship with Mary. He found a security with his wife that he did not find in other relationships. However, he saw Mary as a reflection of his sense of himself rather than as an independent person.

> This is what woman always represents to the imagination of man, a diviner self than his own; a more private, sacred and intimate self than that wherewith nature endows him. (H. James 1870b, 364)

Henry depended on Mary to accept him in a way he could not accept himself. This led him to deny her intelligence and her need for a complex and expressive emotional life. The restriction and denial in Henry's position suggests that his idealization protected him from his ambivalent feelings about being controlled by caretaking figures. His dependency on Mary was possible only when he denied her separateness as a thinking, complex, sexual person. "I have long been used to believe in woman not as sexually, but only as spiritually, pronounced" (H. James 1870a, 67).

Henry and Mary had their first child William in 1842 while they were living at the Astor House in New York City. Henry met Emerson shortly thereafter. The family bought a home in New York, where Henry, Jr., was born the following year. He was still an infant when the family left for Europe.

The James household returned to Albany in 1845. There Henry made a public address to the Young Men's Association on *What Constitutes the State* (1846). The address marked Henry's growing interest in socialism and morality.

Following his trip to Europe and his breakdown, Henry had returned to find American intellectual currents dominated by optimism and idealism. Emerson became Henry's personal guide to this circle of thinkers. Henry's conversion to Swedenborg, which took place during a second prolonged journey to Europe, again carried him away from American idealism to a more conflicted struggle with the relationship between material and spiritual identity. When Henry discovered socialism he believed he had found a way to integrate his concepts with the socialist movements then dominating the thinking of progressive Americans.

Just as Henry had misinterpreted his interest in Emerson's truth, seeking to challenge rather than merely adopt it, he found himself at odds with the socialism of his day. He applied his unusual religious views to politics, arguing that the true state was not the government but man's inherent dependency on other men.

Henry began to lecture in New York and Boston following his experience in Albany. He frequently found himself in the company of Fourier's followers, among them Horace Greeley, Ripley, Godwin, and Dana. Parke Godwin, a friend from divinity school, had written a book which focused on the similarities of the thought of Fourier and Swedenborg. In 1847 both the James family and the *Harbinger* moved to New York, Godwin becoming a principal editor of the journal. There is some indication that Henry began contributing financially to the support of the paper at that time. However, his more theoretical temperament found expression in a different kind of publication.

At the end of 1847 advertisements appeared in the *Harbinger* for a new journal, the *New Times*, of which Henry was to be editor-in-chief. The difference between the journals was to have been one of philosophy rather than contributors, as a majority of those listed were also members of the contributing staff of the *Harbinger*. The *New Times* did not bear any direct relation to Fourier. Its advertisements stated it would be

> for the discussion of the important social, philosophical, and religious questions, which especially agitate the present epoch. The *New Times* will bring to the discussion of these questions, the most catholic spirit, and the light of positive principles. It will aim to maintain in the social sphere, the essential and permanent interest of man; in philosophy, to discover and set forth the laws of order, which govern the spiritual as well as the natural universe; and in religion, to assert and illustrate the distinctive hope of [sic], christianity which is the universal establishment of fraternal relations among men, and the domination of the divine justice on earth. (Warren 1934, 115)

The *New Times* was never published and there is no information as to why it failed. Henry continued his lecturing and began to contribute to the *Harbinger*. Warren summarizes his 32 essays, letters, and reviews:

> He writes on parallels between Fourier and Swedenborg; he attacks the Swedenborgian sect and differs with its doctors; he writes on love and marriage; he discusses the laws of creation and the constitution of human nature; he reviews the tracts which infest the day. (Warren 1934, 113)

In 1849 Emerson arranged for Henry to lecture in Boston by having him become a member of several of the clubs which had been organized among his circle there. In response to a letter inviting him to join and also speak before the Town and Country Club, Henry wrote:

> I am horrified at the prospect of speaking before so urbane an assemblage as I am likely to meet, and nothing but the protection of your magnanimous countenance reconciles me. There is nothing I dread so much as literary men, especially *our* literary men. . . .
> You come to them with some grand secret that opens heaven to the lowest and most excluded hut, that lifts your own life out of bottomless and stifling mud, where living is

abject toil, and expect some involuntary token of human sympathy, even of natural curiosity, — but no, a supercilious smile decks every visage, and the only notice taken of you is a muttered invocation of this, that and the other accepted name.... When a man lives, he can scarcely write. He cannot read, I apprehend, at all. (Perry 1935, I:57–58)

More specifically, Henry's anxiety was about whether his audience would be receptive to a discussion of socialism, the only topic which interested him at that moment, and one which was distinctly identified with his sense of the importance of relationships. His sensitivity to others' reactions to him went hand in hand with his disappointment with American culture. Emerson, he argued, was not an author: "Your books are not literature but life, and criticism always strikes me, therefore, as infinitely laughable when applied to you" (Perry 1935, I:58).

Emerson had an inner congruence which made him confident in himself. Henry felt much more vulnerable: "The fact is, I am in a very bad way I am afraid, for I cannot heartily engage in any topic in which I shall appear to advantage" (Perry 1935, I:59). This as before led him to consider going to Europe:

> Looking upon our four stout boys, who have no play-room within doors, and import shocking bad manners from the street, with much pity, we gravely ponder whether it would not be better to go abroad for a few years with them, allowing them to absorb French and German and get a better sensuous education than they are likely to get here. (Perry 1935, I:59)

Emerson encouraged Henry to speak on socialism and discouraged him from going to Europe. On November 1, 1849, Henry spoke to the Town and Country Club on "Socialism and Civilization in Relation to the Development of the Individual Life." The lecture gave a religious and psychological interpretation to the idea of socialism.

In his letter to Emerson, Henry attributed his wish to go to Europe to a concern for his children's development. He frequently contemplated a European education for them when he was feeling alone in his intellectual struggles. His concerns appear to have been expressions of anxiety in regard to himself. Henry was ambivalent about his own role in American culture. The serenity of Emerson and the intimacy of the Boston club circle dissatisfied him and he felt drawn to his more dramatic European experiences and his sense of special fathering. One response was to give his children an alternative which would also justify his close, self-protective attachment to them.

By 1848 there were three more children in his family. Garth Wilkinson (Wilky) had been born in 1845, Robertson (Bob) in 1846, and Alice in 1848. Henry's moral anxieties concerning them emerged in two areas. The extended family was regarded by him as an empty and shallow world, and school and tutors were found to be inadequate to the needs of the children. During the family's seven comparatively settled years in New York City, from 1847 until 1854, the children were exposed to their father's doubts about their cousins, school life, and American culture.

Henry, Jr., remembered himself as "surrounded by a slightly remote, yet dimly rich, outer and quite kindred circle of the tipsy" (H. James, Jr. [1913] 1956, 29). These "fitful apparitions" (H. James, Jr. [1913] 1956, 29) of unsuccessful and unhappy cousins were elaborated on by their father:

> He regaled us with no scandals, yet it somehow rarely failed to come out that each contemporary on his younger scene, each hero on each thrilling adventure, had, in spite of brilliant promise and romantic charm, ended badly, as badly as possible. (H. James, Jr. [1913] 1956, 29)

In one sense, Henry had internalized the values of *his* father. The dissipating dangers of too much money required an intense sense of morality if one were to survive. The culture provided few creative outlets for the independently wealthy. Its one-dimensional quality was conveyed in Henry, Jr.'s, description of childhood awareness as limited to "three classes, the busy, the tipsy, and Daniel Webster" (H. James, Jr. [1913] 1956, 30).

Henry also found it difficult to tolerate the influence of any particular teacher or school on his children for more than a few months. The children attended

> dispensaries of learning the number and succession of which today excite my wonder; we couldn't have changed oftener, it strikes me as I look back, if our presence had been inveterately objected to. (H. James, Jr. [1913] 1956, 11)

It was not the teachers but their father who made the objections. By 1851 William and Henry, Jr., had studied under five teachers. Henry, Jr., at that time was eight and William nine. This pattern continued throughout their school years.

The children could find security in this world of changing and untrustworthy methods and models by turning to Henry and Mary. Henry used his writing and his family to generate a sense of intimacy and stability in the privacy of his home. His need to retain this security led to an intensification of the disruptive aspects of social life for his children as well as himself.

Henry's disenchantment with social customs caused his children to experience uncertainty and upheaval. Although Henry, Jr., made no complaint about school in this regard (feeling he was saved from a world of striving and competition for which he was unsuited), William did. Henry,

Jr.'s, dissatisfaction emerged when his father refused to identify himself with any particular religious group.

The children were separated from their peers by these unusual practices and felt more vulnerable to criticism from outside the family. Within their close-knit home, however, the peculiarities created a special bond with their father.

In later years Henry also resisted preparing his children in any practical way for careers: "I see him now as fairly afraid to recognise certain anxieties, fairly declining to dabble in the harshness of practical precautions or impositions" (H. James, Jr. [1913] 1956, 126). Truth was sufficient preparation for life and the children were "confirmed in their towniness and fairly enriched in their sensibility, instead of being chucked into a scramble or exposed on breezy uplands under the she-wolf of competition and discipline" (H. James, Jr. [1913] 1956, 127). They were given a sense of being special which could be preserved within the family, but which left them vulnerable to the more competitive and aggressive aspects of American life.

In 1851 Henry scheduled a series of six lectures in Boston on topics including art, property, democracy, and theology. He wrote to Emerson a few days before the lectures were to begin:

> Looking over the lectures again they horrify me with their loud-mouthed imbecility. . . . The fact is that a vital truth can never be transferred from one mind to another, because life alone appreciates it. . . . The reason why the Gods seem so powerless to the sensuous understanding, and suffer themselves to be so long defamed by our crazy theologies, is that they are life, and can consequently be revealed only to life. But life is simply the passage of idea into action. And our crazy theologies forbid ideas to come into action any further than our existing institutions warrant. Hence man leads a mere limping life, and the poor Gods who are dependent upon his manliness for their true revelation, for their real knowledge, are doomed to remain forever unknown. . . . However, I shall try to convert *myself*, at least, into an army of Goths and Huns, to overrun and destroy our existing sanctities, that the supernatural splendours may at length become credible and even visible. (Perry 1935, I:71-72)

Henry interested himself in institutions only insofar as they restricted man from spiritual salvation. His battle with morality placed him on the side of the uncivilized, the Goths and Huns. Change was not a matter of intellectualizing, of books and critical comment, but of life and aliveness.

Henry was terrified of delivering this message, feeling that the formalities of his audience would lead them to reject him. He identified his own anxieties with theirs as he described the "mere limping life" of most men, merging an image of himself as physically crippled with one of them as spiritually crippled. Civilized man limped. He and his audience had to find a more primitive means of expression for their emotional lives. Like the Goths and Huns, they had to overrun false civilization.

Inward understanding required Henry to be passive, to sit and allow himself to experience his terror. The resolution to this was not to create new institutions but to accept his inner life. In order to enlarge and enliven this inner life he had to destroy the restrictions of the civilized intellect. As a kind of negative crusader he challenged others to let go of the institutional realities and moralisms by which they lived and seek the spiritual voice within them.

The experience of sharing a different and more personal kind of reality and in this way making his inner world vulnerable to public scrutiny apparently exhausted Henry. He terminated his Boston lectures early, pleading ill health, and went back to the safety of preparing his books. Within the close-knit family and among friends such as Emerson his spirituality was more comfortable.

Emerson was particularly disappointed in this flight:

> But you are a grievous sinner, and I hope your great sin, ere this, cut you to the heart. It is only a half-expiation — your printing and publishing. And the book will not be as good as if you had exposed it fully to our northern air. I have never been able to reach a more than Thomasian faith in the acute disease which drove you from Boston. (Perry 1935, I:73)

In 1854 Henry published his third book, *The Church of Christ Not an Ecclesiasticism, A Letter to a Sectarian*. This book, an attack on the Swedenborgian sect, won Emerson's warm praise. The following year Henry published *The Nature of Evil* (1855). He argued that evil and selfishness were part of God's benevolent plan. The book sold well. Henry wrote to Emerson:

> I have one astonishment to give you, which is, that the whole edition — 1000 copies — is exhausted. To think of a book of that dullness as to subject, and that *thereforeiness* as to treatment, being sold to this extent in four months, gives one new hope in humanity. I may yet perhaps be mentioned with Emerson, Dickens, Thackeray, Carlyle, and other popular authors. (Perry 1935, I:81)

Success renewed Henry's anxiety. Rather than pursuing his possibilities, he left shortly afterward with his family for Europe.

Henry's flight following the success of his book suggests that he needed the privacy of his literary work as an alternative to the more vulnerable aspects of his identity as a lecturer. Despite his desire to become a popular writer he wrote essentially for himself. Having lost some of the protectiveness of his literary world, he created a different kind of space for himself and his family by going to Europe.

Europe

On June 27, 1855, the James family left on a three-year journey to Europe. They landed in Liverpool, stopped briefly in London, went to Paris and then to Geneva where Henry planned to have his children educated. The Geneva schools were considered among the best organized and most progressive in Europe.

Henry's initial enthusiasm for Geneva's schools and his subsequent withdrawal of his children from them were reported in his letters. In the New York *Daily Tribune* he expressed particular enthusiasm for the Presbyterianism of Geneva, noting Calvin's decision to build an educational institution which "aspired to give theology a scientific footing" (Le Clair 1955, 160). This contrasted to the more rigid and limited schooling and religion of his youth. The focus on outdoor life and good health also earned his praises. Henry was impressed by the noncommercial focus of the educational process and commented on its moral advantages.

> Certainly it is very lovely to see youth preserving its ingenuousness; to see boyhood wholly unused to the coarse and brutal commerce of the great world; and from all I can learn I really think these schools do everything possible to secure that advantage. (Le Clair 1955, 162)

This enthusiastic report, written August 13, 1855, was followed on September 25 by a letter to Henry's mother suggesting that even these idyllic surroundings were not sufficient for his children:

> We are living on comfortably enough here in Geneva, but have come to the conclusion that the schools are greatly over-rated. We do not find the advantages we had expected in them; or rather we did not anticipate the sacrifices by which in respect especially to the younger children, these advantages are to be bought. They have enjoyment enough, and live better than is common with these schools, but Mary never sees them without feeling how much they need her personal care, and how little they get in exchange for the lack. We have come to the conclusion that home tuition will be the best for all of them; that while it will be much the least expensive, it will also be greatly to the interest of the children both in moral and intellectual regards. (Le Clair 1955, 171)

The initial excitement of Europe had worn off and Mary and Henry felt the need to have their children at home. In October the family headed back to Paris, and then to London.

The parental preoccupation with the family unit as the source of all trustworthy moral development suggests a continuation in Europe of Henry's preoccupation with security. Henry, Jr., later wrote of his father as using the family environment as a means of feeling safe in what was otherwise a strange and frightening world. After his trips to other European cities

Henry would describe to his children the "horrid inhuman inns" and "hard alien races" which could never replace the family circle (H. James, Jr. [1913] 1956, 43).

> He reacted, he rebounded, in favour of his fireside, from whatever brief explorations or curiosities; these passionate spontaneities were the pulse of his life and quite some of the principal events of ours; and, as he was nothing if not expressive, whatever happened to him for inward intensity happened abundantly to us for pity and terror, as it were, as well as for an ease and a quality of amusement among ourselves that was really always to fail us among others. (H. James, Jr. [1913] 1956, 43)

Henry's choice of his children as his very close companions provided him with an experience of deep caring, something more stabilizing than social recognition. It left his children with an unrealistic sense of the relationship between the family and the social world. The family seemed to be the only safe place for their father and for them.

Just as schools had threatened this unusual family intimacy by removing the children from their parents' influence, tutors could easily distract the children's attention from their parents. No tutors or governesses were ever satisfactory to Henry, and they continued to come and go with characteristic frequency. It is difficult to know whether anyone could have measured up to his high standards without at the same time threatening the closeness which centered on his role in the family.

Financial restrictions led the James family to Boulogne in the summer of 1857. During that summer Alice became aware of the central moral lesson of the family, the issue of vulnerability and how one came to terms with it. Her insight was sparked by a visit to the family of her governess:

> Marie told us that her father had a scar upon his face caused by a bad scald in his youth and we must be sure and not look at him as he was very sensitive. How I remember the painful conflict between sympathy and the desire to look and the fear that my baseness should be discovered by the good man.... How easy 'twould be to picture one's youth as a perpetual escape from that abhorred object! — I wonder if it is a blight upon children still? (A. James 1965, 128)

Alice's desire to look suggests that she was curious about the experience of being physically damaged. Her father, like her governess's father, had suffered a severe burn in childhood and subsequent debility. Both men were very sensitive.

Alice must have wished to take a good hard look at her father's injury, his sexuality, and his sensitivity, all of which to her young mind seemed linked. Such an activity was prohibited by her governess because it would be shocking and upsetting. Alice was confronted by both the wish to see her father's experience and the fear that in doing so she would upset him. The form of escape which she discovered that same day was intellectualization. It allowed one to be moral; that is, to express one's wishes and fears in a way that did not hurt others.

> But to arrive, at the first flowering of my Intellect! . . . Harry was sitting in the swing and I came up and stood nearby as the sun began to slant over the desolate expanse, as the dreary h[ou]rs, with that endlessness which they have for infancy, passed, when Harry suddenly exclaimed: "This might certainly be called pleasure under difficulties!" The stir of my whole being in response to the substance and exquisite, *original* form of this remark almost makes my heart beat now with sisterly pride which was then awakened and it came to me in a flash, the higher nature of this appeal to the mind, as compared to the rudimentary solicitations which usually produced my childish explosions of laughter; and I can feel distinctly the sense of self-satisfaction in that I could not only perceive, but appreciate this subtlety, as if I had acquired a new sense, a sense whereby to measure intellectual things, wit as distinguished from giggling, for example. (A. James 1965, 128-29)

Avoiding her father because he had become the "abhorred object" of her curiosity would have left Alice in a state of emotional desolation. Henry, Jr., introduced her to a humorous intellectual perspective on one's experience as another form of control. This allowed one to acknowledge discomfort while keeping one's curiosity in check. Rather than staring her injured father in the eye and possibly hurting his feelings, she might seek intellectual understanding. Rather than giggle like a little girl at her father's ideas and his pain she could begin to adopt the family preoccupation with mental life.

With varying degrees of success the children internalized the values which their father portrayed. Having a relationship with him meant sharing Henry's sense of "pleasure under difficulties" (A. James 1965, 128). Family intimacy could be fun and comforting, but the world at large was a dangerous place. Alice's later illnesses captured the contradictory messages she and her brothers received. She described her experience as one of maintaining control, but at great cost. Her next journal entry after the memory of Boulogne began, "How well one has to be, to be ill!" (A. James 1965, 128).

In the James family, emotional illness and health were inseparably bound together. For Henry, pain and vulnerability justified turning away from the world to the support of one's family and the ultimate comfort of God's love. One could not experience Henry's love without sharing his unhappiness. Maturity meant mastering this unhappiness by accepting his intellectualized demands for intimacy, framed as moral precepts about the dangers of growing up. Just to be a child without confronting such serious issues meant isolating oneself from the central dynamics of the family. The family's social isolation made this practically impossible.

In Boulogne, Henry, Jr., became severely ill with typhus. The illness and his prolonged recovery overwhelmed him with "strange pains and apprehensions" (H. James [1913] 1956, 236). One of these apprehensions may well have been his awareness that his father was devoting increasingly more of his attention to William's moral development. Henry appears to have turned away from Henry, Jr., at this time of illness. He wrote to his mother:

> Harry, I am thankful to say is doing very well, having but one serious pull-back. . . . Willy is very devoted to scientific pursuits, and I hope will turn out a most respectable scholar. He has been attending the College Imperial here all summer, and one of his professors told me the other day "that he was an admirable student, and that all the advantages of a first-rate scientific education which Paris affords ought to be accorded him." He is, however, much dearer to my heart for his moral worth than for his intellectual. I never knew a child of so much principle, and at the same time of a perfectly generous and conciliatory demeanour towards his younger brothers, always disposed to help them and never to oppress. (Perry 1935, I:184)

The letter continues:

> Harry is not so fond of study, properly so-called, as of reading. He is a devourer of libraries, and an immense writer of novels and dramas. He has considerable talent as a writer, but I am at a loss to know whether he will ever accomplish much. . . . Wilkie has more heart than head, but has a talent for language, and speaks French they say with a perfect accent. They all speak very fluently indeed but Wilkie and Bob (who is clever and promising, having ten times the go-ahead of all the rest) are particularly forward in it. Alice also speaks very well, and I presume that this winter will greatly accomplish them. (Strouse 1980, 57)

Although all the children except Henry, Jr., seem to have pleased their father, William was clearly the child who had succeeded in the crucial area of morality. He began to hold a special place in his father's eyes. This was enhanced by his growing interest in science.

The Christmas before his 17th birthday, William was given a microscope by his father.

> William happened upon the bill for it in advance, and was hardly able to contain his excitement until Christmas day, so portentous seemed the impending event. Apparently no similar experience ever equalled the intensity of this one. (W. James 1920, I:21)

Henry may have characteristically decided that by giving William a microscope he was exposing him to all the tools necessary for a scientific education, as William's professor had recommended. A scientific education in Paris would have involved leaving William by himself in a school, which the parents had already shown themselves reluctant to do in Geneva.

The passage introducing the issue of William's scientific talents continues by focusing on his moral worth. If Henry considered separating William from the family, he may have decided not to do so based on this issue. He justified keeping the family intact by pointing to the importance of William's influence on his younger siblings, his "generous and conciliatory demeanor." This influence may have been most pronounced in the relationship between William and his father. Willam's acceptance of his father's expectations of him gave his father a sense of his moral value.

In fact William's relationship with his brothers was not particularly protective. His interest in science led him to experiment with chemicals, photography, and electricity, with occasional accidents and explosions. These earned the irritation of his mother and his brothers.

In July 1858 the family returned briefly to the United States. They settled in Newport. Henry considered moving to Cambridge and enrolling William in the Scientific School at Harvard. By September 1859 he had decided to return to Europe instead. He again explained his decision as involving the moral development of his children.

> I have grown so discouraged about the education of my children here, and dread so their inevitable habits of extravagance and insubordination, which appear to be the characteristics of American youth, that I have come to the conclusion to retrace my steps to Europe, and keep them there a few years longer. . . . At all accounts, I am quite sure that my main object in life, which is to do justice to my children, will be so promoted by our return to Europe, as to make all my lesser activities and obligations easily fulfilled. (Le Clair 1955, 291-92)

Despite his protests of self-sacrifice, the "inevitable habits of extravagance and insubordination" which Henry found so displeasing reflected his continuing need to maintain especially close contact with his children. As the children began to develop other relationships he began to feel uncertain as to their moral development. He jealously guarded his spiritual influence over them.

This may have particularly been an issue in the summer of 1859, when William and Henry, Jr., began to spend time with the artist John LaFarge. Henry may have sensed William's growing interest in art, a pursuit which led him away from his father's expectations that he would become a scientist.

The family returned to Geneva in October 1859. The children attended boarding schools in Switzerland while Henry traveled to Paris and London. In the summer of 1860 the James family, minus Bob, went to Germany. Shortly after arriving William, then 18, announced to his father that he had decided to study art. This led Henry to reconsider his plans to stay on in

Germany. He decided to return to the United States in September. He wrote to a friend:

> But we had hardly reached here before Willy took an opportunity to say to me—what it seems he had been long wanting to say, but found it difficult to come to the scratch—that he felt the vocation of a painter so strongly that he did not think it worth my while to expend any more time or money on his scientific education! I confess I was greatly startled by the annunciation, and not a little grieved, for I had always counted upon a scientific career for Willy, and I hope the day may even yet come when my calculations may be realized in this regard. But as it was I had nothing to do but submit; and as our motive to stay in Europe was chiefly derived from the imagined needs of his education, so now we are glad enough to turn homewards, and let him begin at once with Mr. Hunt. The welfare of the other youngsters will, however, be as much consulted by this manoeuvre, I am persuaded, as Willy's. They are none of them cut out for intellectual labours, and they are getting to an age, Harry and Wilky especially, when the heart craves a little wider expansion than is furnished by the domestic affections. They want friends among their own sex, and sweethearts in the other; and my hope for their own salvation, temporal and spiritual, is that they may "go it strong" in both lines when they get home. (Perry 1935, I:191)

Henry dealt with his disappointment in William by depreciating the intellectual abilities of his younger children and giving in to William's demands. His high estimation of William's moral worth was not shaken by his son's rebellion. He justified the plan to move back to the United States by finding value in the possibility of increasing social contacts for the younger children, and by denying any significant loss he may have felt in regard to William's disinterest in science.

In the autumn of 1860 the family returned to Newport, ending their European travels. Henry concluded in a letter announcing their return:

> My sole hope for humanity is that men will go on more and more to such a complete obedience of their natural instincts, that all our futile old rulers, civil and religious, will grow so bewildered as to abandon their thrones and leave the coast clear to scientific men. (Perry 1935, I:192)

This seems to have been his wish for William. Let him rebel, Henry implied, and although by doing so he makes one feel like a "futile old ruler," the chaos will lead him to science.

Henry had temporarily lost control over William's moral development. He constructed an intellectual explanation of William's actions with the outcome the result he had hoped for. Six days later he wrote to the same friend:

> I hoped that his career would be a scientific one, as I thought and still think that the true bent of his genius was towards the acquisition of knowledge: and to give up this hope

without a struggle, and allow him to tumble down into a mere painter, was impossible. (Perry 1935, I:192)

Henry described his investment in William as a deliberate experiment. However, the family had initially moved to Newport after Henry had been told of William's scientific potential. In Newport Henry had been less involved with his children, traveling frequently and allowing his children to develop friendships outside the family. Perhaps without realizing it he had encouraged William's interest in a new tutor at an age which was not far from his age at the time of his own relationship with Joseph Henry. Henry's behavior at this time resembled that of his own uninvolved father. Being back in America led to an experience for his children of growing up much as he had in a less isolated environment. He subjected William to the test of having new relationships from which to develop a sense of identity. He was now having to face the fact that William had been attracted by this experience and had chosen an artist rather than a scientist as a model.

Henry's motivations in pushing William toward science and away from art can be traced in part to his relationship with Joseph Henry. Joseph had been a support for Henry following his injury and again after he was punished in his father's will. A man who had combined a brilliant scientific career with an open-minded attitude toward new religious ideas, he was perhaps the model that Henry had in mind as he encouraged William to pursue a scientific career.

Henry turned to William in hopes that William's scientific interests would make America safe for him and guarantee his son a successful adulthood. When William developed an interest in art Henry quickly took him back to Europe. Finally at William's insistence, Henry allowed his son to pursue his artistic interests. He did so, however, by taking the family back to Newport. He by no means gave up on his plans for his son. Henry expressed the hope that the controls which science had once provided in his life would again guarantee a successful transition into adulthood. In this case the transition would be William's.

William did in fact renounce art after several months of study. He enrolled in the Harvard Scientific School as his father had hoped. In 1864 he transferred to the Medical School. His capacity to meet his father's hopes for a special intellectual closeness are discussed in chapter 4.

3
Father's Ideas

The Inner World

Henry was a devoted father and an equally devoted writer. "'Father's ideas,'" wrote Henry, Jr., "pervaded and supported his existence and very considerably our own" (H. James, Jr. [1914] 1956, 330).

Henry, Jr., accurately observed that his father's obscure ideas about the self and society paralleled his family experience. Initially he focused on the value of self-expression and spontaneity at the expense of relationships, issues which allowed him to work out his feelings toward his father. As he matured, his close relationships with his children became more crucial and his ideas reflected this change.

There is an obvious parallel between Henry's philosophical interest in introspection and his childhood and adolescent conflicts concerning religion and paternal authority. The sudden and short-lived interest which his father showed toward him following his accident intensified his tendency to idealize and his need to test the validity of his idealizations. The former provided him with a religious temperament while the latter led to severe and recurring crises of belief during his early adulthood.

Henry entered into a final crisis of belief at the age of 33, which he resolved by developing an identity as a theological writer. Although his theories retained many of the qualities of religious thought and style, they eventually moved beyond a theocentric concept of the universe. Henry continued to think and write about God, but he slowly shifted his primary focus to the introspective and creative capacities of man.

Central to all of Henry's writing and his experience is the inherent coherence of the inner world when contrasted with the fragmentary qualities of external experience. Henry's theory focused exclusively on the inner dynamics of experience. Man's inner world is most important because it reflects God's presence and is the only way man can know God. Man is real only through his experience of this inner world: "The internal of every man is God. The external, or that which defines the man, defines his self-consciousness, is only a shadow or reflection of the internal" (H. James 1850, 6).

Henry constructs a hierarchy. God is being. Man is "the shadow or image of God . . . the reflection of being" (H. James 1850, 6). Nature is phenomenal, or real only insofar as it gives man an experience of separateness from God. Nature, which most men believe to be the basis of awareness, is illusion. All that we think of as externally present is in fact the least real and reliable component of our knowledge.

The confused, fragmentary, and unstable sensory world requires inner emotional experience to provide unity and security in life. Each dimension of the "created universe" (H. James 1850, 7) corresponds to some element of the active, perceiving spiritual reality and derives its meaning through the connection. Man, who is both physical and spiritual, is the object as well as the subject of this creation. His is "a composite self-hood" (H. James 1850, 13). Since man has identity, he must "possess an internal or spiritual self as the end or object of the action, and an external self as its means or instrument" (H. James 1850, 13).

Man's fragmentary experience is explained as the product of two kinds of awareness. The first, which is spiritual, functions like a mirror reflecting God's true creative power. Religion gives meaning to daily life as a mirror reflects light or a shadow gives form but not substance to a shape. Meaning comes from God. In his actions man appropriates God's love and endows his life with meaning. But he does not in this way give true being to the natural world or to his sense of self. Its function remains symbolic; it gives man his knowledge of God.

The second form of understanding lies in the experience of nature and history. Natural and social actions require man to subject himself to physical and moral laws. Society and nature alienate man from his spiritual and reflective capacities yet also force him to acknowledge that these capacities are not his own but are reflections of God's true being. Nature and history thus provide man with a crucial experience of alienation, a sense of separateness from God.

Self-Expression

At the earliest stage of his thought Henry places most credence on the artistic unification and expression of man's state. The divine man "unites in himself, or harmonizes" (H. James 1850, 24) the conflictual tensions of natural, social, and spiritual life. In order to do this he must respond only to the "immortal beauty whose presence constitutes his inmost soul" (H. James 1850, 25). The artist "is a law unto himself, and ignores all outward allegiance, whether to nature or society" (H. James 1850, 27). Aesthetic expression does not mean conforming to principles of art but turning one's divine vision into a natural form.

In order to express the divine, a man must isolate himself from society; that is, from relationships. The inner world which Henry describes is characterized by its isolation. Man cannot reach God in any direct sense but only experience Him reflectively. Yet to do this he must separate himself from the worlds of nature and society.

The loneliness implied by this formulation is countered by a focus on action:

> Our true individuality is our faculty of action, our power to do. By so much as I am able to do or produce, am I myself. A man *is* that which he *does*, neither more nor less. What I do, that I am. I possess both passion and intelligence, but neither of these things characterize *me*; they characterize all men, characterize my nature. What characterizes me, what gives me individuality, or distinctive genius, is my action. Thus all character is grounded in action; all being grounded in doing; all cause grounded in effect. (H. James 1850, 48)

Action distinguishes man from other men and should give him true identity or being. Yet it must be action which is spontaneous and tasteful, not obedience to social customs and constraints.

> All action properly so called, all action which really individualizes us, is essentially aesthetic. Not our physical and moral action, or what we do from the constraint of necessity and duty, but only our aesthetic action, or what we do from taste, from spontaneity, expresses our true or inmost personality. (H. James 1850, 49)

The concept of spontaneous individual action is contradictory. Creativity is described as effortless spontaneity. This is man's way of knowing God, whose being is reflected in man's creative awareness. However Henry has developed a theology in which there is no externally existing God but only a reflection of God in man's spiritual experience. In this way he has written in a manner which parallels his experience with his father, a presence whose physical absence was counterbalanced by an overpowering emotional impact. Henry's religious emotions are in fact so intense that God's physical absence seems immaterial.

Such a theology suggests loneliness and confusion. Henry's deepest religious emotions appear to be feelings of despair. What is real in this conceptual sphere is not an effort to communicate but a compensation for disappointment through action and expression. God cannot reveal himself to the inadequate, fragmented, natural man except by a longing which man feels. Man looks at the shadow of his physical experience and longs for something more substantial. He looks at the constraints of social life and longs to do as he pleases. In this way he presumably learns about divinity and freedom. But freedom of action, having not made God real to man's experience, can no more make man real to himself.

Henry's theory of spontaneous action hides his longing to act in a way that will dramatize his loneliness. This obscures the possibility of expressing pain and vulnerability:

> The only man whom nature respects, though she has at present a very imperfect respect for any man, the only man whom she feeds with her choicest juices and aromas, is the man who cares not a jot about her, and snaps his fingers equally at her curse and her blessing. (H. James 1850, 51)

Henry struggles with this idea of spontaneous man whose indifference might well be seen as hiding deep anger at the hostility of nature and society toward his needs. From Henry's perspective, activity is this isolated and self-sufficient man's way to salvation. As he continues the passage it becomes evident that he uses action as protection from emotional turmoil:

> So let me devote myself, with a view to life, to the fulfilling of the moral law, or the complete discharge of my obligations to my fellow-man, and instead of the life I covet, ten thousand deaths instantly open their mouths to sting me into despair and madness. (H. James 1850, 52)

So long as he regards the indifferent world with equal indifference he is isolated but secure. However any attempt to assume a social identity leads not to the feeling of life for which he had hoped but to guilt and despair.

The contradiction between man's spontaneity and the indifferent and eventually hostile tendencies of the world must be explained without excluding the idea of a benevolent God. Henry enmeshes his entire explanation into a single extended sentence:

> The letter of the law appears brief and easy, but the moment I indulge the fatal anxiety, have I fulfilled it? I begin to apprehend its infinite spirit, the spirit of benevolence or charity, which prompts such an utter crucifixion of selfishness—such an incessant and immaculate deference to the will and even the whimsy of another, that I am worried and fretted into my grave, before I have really entered on my obedience—and the law which I fondly deemed to intend me life, turns out a minister of utter death. (H. James 1850, 51-52)

Henry conceptualizes a function for social law which justifies his unhappiness. The spirit of the law like nature points out man's limitations. Morality undermines spontaneous action by awakening the person to his capacity for self-evaluation and its related anxieties. The natural world gives way to a sense of responsibility, and thus to terror: "the sentiment of responsibility grinds human life into the dust" (H. James 1850, 60).

Society and social regulations become a target for Henry's frustration with a God who could not appear in any tangible form. This focus removes Henry from the ranks of the usual religious mystic who seeks a more direct relationship with God by renouncing physical and social reality and the conflict inherent in it.

Society and the Self

The issue of vulnerability preoccupies Henry as he addresses the relationship between society and the individual. The social roles through which an approved sense of self are expressed provide only false security:

> The error of society herein lies in its giving man what Swedenborg calls a *false proprium*, that is a property which God does not give him. Society does all it can to finite man, to include or shut up his proprium, his selfhood, within itself, and so render him its abject vassal or dependent. . . . God, on the contrary, seeks incessantly to aggrandize His child, and render him *in-finite*. (H. James 1850, 66)

In the conflict between religious and social identity, society takes an active rather than a merely passive role. In his earlier writing, the images of spiritual being and aesthetic expression were more fully separated from social experience, which was regarded as important only as a reflection of spiritual life. Later Henry sees society as taking a position in relation to spiritual life, endowing it with an image of property; that is, regarding the soul as something on whose purity man is dependent if he is to be saved. This argument is the basis for the assumption that the existing church is essentially a secular, and not a religious, institution. It represents the interests of social control rather than spiritual growth. The church acts for society in its restrictions on the behavior of its members. It gives those who accept its morality a false sense of pride in themselves and a sense of superiority to others. True religion, on the other hand, gives men a sense of humility and of identification with all of man, or Divine Natural Humanity. Society regards identity as the product of social expression. For Henry, this is a painful and false solution.

The emptiness Henry experiences in trying to find meaning in society suggests the need for different kinds of relationships. He proposes socialism, which "reveals the incessant operation of laws by which man's physical and social relations will be brought into the complete subjection of his inward or divine personality" (H. James 1850, 83). By integrating spiritual knowledge into relationships man can construct a society in which meaning triumphs over performance. There is then no need to conceal the anxieties of personal life from social interaction.

> If I am one with nature and my fellowman, if there be a sovereign unity and not enmity pervading all our reciprocal relations, then clearly every appetite and affection both of my physical and moral nature become instantly legitimated, and I stand henceforth absolved from all defilement, a new creature of God triumphant over death and hell, nay more, taking death and hell into friendly subjection, and suffusing their hitherto dusk and dejected visages with the roseate flush of omnipresent and omnipotent Life. (H. James 1850, 84)

Man can accept and integrate his moral and natural selves if there is an ideal society in which relationships are based on spiritual principles. Ideal society is described as acting in contrast to the more primitive feeling of self-love which predominates in childhood.

So long as social norms can be viewed as the extension of parental influence, both benevolent and authoritarian, then there is no need to theorize about a possible society which extends beyond their limits. For Henry, however, the absence of a definitive relationship with his father led him to imagine a more intense form of fellowship. When his early idealizations became empty, his new vision of society endowed his identity with meaning, allowing him to leave behind his childhood naivete:

> Nature subjects me to the operation of self-love by the various stimulants it offers to my sense, leading me to seek their continual and highest possible gratification. Society, or the fellowship of my kind, subjects me to the equal operations of charity or neighborly love, by the various incitements it offers to my affections, leading me to seek *their* continual and highest possible gratification. (H. James 1850, 103)

When the two sets of forces of ideal self and ideal society are in balance, one is freed to become conscious of one's spiritual life. Acknowledgment of the infinite, however, must begin by rejection of the finite. Natural and social life must be seen as "inevitably finite or imperfect" (H. James 1850, 106). In the battle to overcome the natural tendencies of self-expression, both social institutions and artistic sensibilities tend to be aggrandized. One must focus on their restrictive definitions of human experience in the absence of a caring society.

Society in its present unfinished form tends to foster a rigid notion of identity. Rebellion and despair in response to this are signs of an active spiritual life.

> It is only because society denies me a consciousness of unity with God, by obstinately limiting my unity with nature and man, that I become tortured with the conscience of sin. . . .
> . . . Thus it is not the moral life which is hurtful, but only the stupid pride and self-complacency with which we view our attainments in that direction. (H. James 1850, 153–58)

In *Lectures and Miscellanies* (1852), Henry explored his growing feeling of possible connectedness with an ideal society. This led him to discuss interaction and unification rather than isolation and confusion.

> Man knows and can know nothing of the facts of his inner or spiritual being, until they become reproduced in nature, until they become fixed or embodied in act. We know nothing in respect either to the nature or the intensity of our passions until they become developed in action.... And this is for a very good reason, namely, that power, no matter of what sort, has no passive existence, has no existence apart from performance. Power in other words is purely active. It is never power save in producing. (H. James 1852, 64–65)

Henry's identification with his father had begun to coalesce in a more satisfying way. The spiritual power of love symbolizes Henry's need for that relationship. It captures his intense wish for his father's active support. This is what Henry sought to sustain as he developed his theology in a way which incorporated society.

By focusing on action in society, Henry also captures an image of his father's financial genius. Finance and power were the tools with which William of Albany constructed his social world. Henry's focus on action suggests transformation rather than isolation. In this way he developed a more realistic understanding of William of Albany's identity and influence.

Although Henry continues to describe spontaneous spiritual vision, he begins to view it as having social meaning. The artist must "show nature and society everywhere pregnant with meaning, everywhere pervaded by a human soul" (H. James 1852, 125). Art is joined by science, which places spontaneity within society, binding it more clearly to social thought.

In traditional theology, creation was the arbitrary act of a "fixed will" (H. James 1852, 154). This left man with no role but that of an "insecure" (H. James 1852, 154) observer whose existence was dependent on whim. In Henry's theology, however, creation is viewed as "an operation rather of the essential perfection of God, an outgrowth of his very selfhood" (H. James 1852, 155). The power of creation, like that of relationships, is intrinsic rather than extrinsic. Man participates in God's creative power rather than merely observing it. Man's consciousness is transformed from passive compliance to good and evil to an active participation in God's monistic goodness.

> Conscience, or the knowledge of good and evil, is a phenomenon which marks the infancy of human culture. It has its origin in the limitation which the senses impose upon the infantile consciousness of man. For the ... senses ... impose upon man a limitary consciousness, the consciousness of a selfhood limited by his own body and by his fellow-man.

> But a profound instinct of the soul wages eternal war with this finite consciousness. The soul of man incessantly affirms a positive good, or a good unlimited by any evil, affirms a positive light, or a light without any oppugnancy or darkness; affirms a positive life, or a life which is without any contrast or antagonism of death. (H. James 1852, 168-69)

Henry has integrated action into his idealism, and this action has found its role in human society as science and power. He conceptualizes the humanness of God's presence, the social reality of caring. In his earlier writings, this caring appeared only as an isolated vision of an idealized invulnerable figure.

The active process of caring is contrasted to the ideal image of a caring figure in traditional theology, in which man is the passive child. Similarly Henry's socialism may be contrasted to the earlier image of spontaneous individuality.

> To love and to know — passion and intellect — such is the ordinary programme of human destiny. But this is to leave out the divinest feature of manhood, that of life or power.... The love I feel which is denied expression, is only a torment to me. The wisdom I have mastered, unless it go forth into exercise, is no better than folly.... Power and not passion, ability and not knowledge, is the crowning or divine mark of manhood. (H. James 1852, 282-83)

Henry has arrived at a quite complex synthesis of spiritual and physical forces in humanity. Time, space, and action have been integrated into an ideal conception of creation. Special care is taken to prevent these natural and moral forces from dominating his system, for they have been relegated to a position which is "phenomenal" rather than real. Science provides a means of subjecting nature and society to man's creative capacities and thus the inner life dominates yet finds expression in social existence.

Psychologically Henry has moved from confusion and isolation to synthesis and integration. His system reflects his continuing need to maintain a sense of protection from the traumatic, uncertain world of experience, which includes imagery of damnation for the natural sense of self. He has, on the other hand, a sense of spiritual identity.

The Experience of Relationships

In his intermediary books (1855, 1857, 1863), which present his ideas in a philosophical context, Henry essentially reviews and redefines the processes presented in his earlier books, using philosophy rather than action as his central concern. This focus on philosophy is paralleled by a greater interest in consciousness. He defines the limitations of consciousness, using this concept to distinguish between thought and spontaneity and thus between God's presence in human nature and man's response to that presence:

> Thus time and space do not exist in themselves (or apart from the mind), but only relatively to the human subject; the all of time representing the bounds, thus the integrity, of human thought; the all of space the bounds, thus the integrity, of human passion: so both alike compelling, the one all history, the other all existence, within the strictest limits of the human form, within the straitest dimensions of the human consciousness. (H. James 1863, 70)

God's eternal presence is experienced by man through the natural phenomena of space and time, and the mental phenomena of thought and passion. Consciousness is not an individual experience but a characteristic of human nature. Social relationships are considered in the context of consciousness rather than science and activity.

Consciousness allows Henry to discuss despair in addition to mastery. By separating man's thought from God's spontaneous influence he is able to explain the simultaneous feelings of alienation and a caring relationship:

> But so long as we have only natural organs, we must needs report every inner accession of life we experience in these broken accents of natural despair and death: or else be wholly misunderstood. No one in such a case has the least intention to intimate that God feels towards him the same condemnation he feels towards himself. He knows the contrary. He knows in all his bones that God feels infinitely more tenderness towards him than He feels towards Himself; and can by no possibility feel otherwise to all eternity. (H. James 1863, 186)

Consciousness is man's attempt to unite what sensory experience presents as separate. Yet without the fragmentary, disruptive experience of sensation man would not have an existence independent from God, that is, from his feeling of relatedness. Without such a separation "irreparable damage and confusion must ensue in the infinite becoming finite, and the finite infinite" (H. James 1863, 386).

This issue articulates for the first time the frightening dimension to Henry's experience with his father, his wish to remain separate from relationships and his fear of being engulfed and destroyed by his father's power. On a theoretical level he has begun to accept the distance he felt from his father. Despite the intensity of his wish to retain a close, protective, and intense connection with his father, he also senses the potential loss of his own autonomy in such a situation.

This provides an important explanation for Henry's idealization of the relationship. The idealization both perpetuated and limited his relationship with his father. It gave him a sense of more control, despite the fragmentary and uncertain quality of that control. His ideas, however unclear, were safer methods of experiencing his father's closeness than was the uncertain and overwhelming direct experience.

Only by withdrawing could William of Albany provide Henry with the necessary space to develop his own identity:

> If the creature should not consciously exist; if he should not possess finite form or selfhood, he would obviously be destitute of identity, could not be said to be, and neither creation nor anything else could be predicated of him. To create means to give being or communicate life to what assuredly is not oneself; and if this be so the creator is bound in order to impart His own being or communicate Himself to the creature, above all things else to posit the creature, or afford him some adequate and veracious ground of self-consciousness. (H. James 1863, 400–401)

It is the sponsoring love of the creator which inspires him to subject his creature to despair and a feeling of abandonment. History calls for suffering and frustration. Otherwise there can be no sense of life in the creature.

Alienation is no longer regarded as an indication of God's hatred and punishment, as Henry had believed as a child, but as God's consideration of man's separate needs. The creator is perfect "without any fellowship. His unity is so absolute as to exclude all community" (H. James 1863, 413). Man's imperfections lead him to seek the opposite of unity, or community, a shared historical and social experience. To express one's "essential dependence" (H. James 1863, 414) is to satisfy the creator's plan for man. Henry has expressed his need for isolation in his image of God's relationship to man. He is then able to accept his dependence on other people without endowing it with totalistic expectations. Philosophy, in explaining religion and despair, replaces science, which had focused his capacities to master the world of his overwhelming physical needs.

In *The Secret of Swedenborg* (1869), Henry begins by presenting a dualistic concept of consciousness. He establishes the primacy of spiritual awareness over natural experience. Consciousness must integrate the two, making man cognizant of both his humanity and his uniqueness. The mechanism by which man gains this consciousness involves a relationship with God. Love in human nature becomes more central as this relationship between man and God is more complete:

> Love of its own nature, of its own fulness or perfection, tends *to create*, i.e., tends *not to be in itself*, but only in forms created from itself to which it may thus communicate its own eternal felicities. It tends to forget itself, to abandon itself, to lose or merge itself in whatsoever is not love, but self; just as self, in its turn, becoming thus incited or vivified, tends of its proper nature, of its proper want or imperfection, *to be loved* infinitely, i.e., tends to seek itself and find itself in whatsoever is not itself, namely, infinite love. And this reciprocal tendency of love to be finited by not-love or self, and of self to be infinited by not-self or love, results logically in the universe of creation which we call nature. (H. James 1869, 34)

This love finds "its supreme felicity in *communicating* itself to others created from itself, in whom it may be and forever abide as in itself" (H. James 1869, 41).

In focusing on the nature of love rather than the self, Henry suggests that there has been some resolution of the experience of his childhood. He has found a means of experiencing and expressing the sponsoring love which had for some time been only a spiritual vision. His theoretical work was instrumental in resolving this problem.

Another crucial element may have come from Henry's actual experiences with his family. In his efforts to be a more real force in the lives of his children than his father had been, he began to experience a more solid feeling about relationships and their importance, accepting closeness as a part of identity formation.

Henry experienced an ongoing intensity with his children that was absent from his life as a child. In this way he actualized his feelings toward his father. He experienced the spontaneity and meaningful activity he discussed in his writing. The creator's self-denying love became especially important for him because it clarified this transition from isolation to dependency.

Creation became "an utter, total, unstinted self-abnegation (as it must always appear to our selfish intelligence) on the part of the infinite love" (H. James 1869, 52).

With this sense of love, the satisfactions of consciousness were replaced by those of revelation:

> Revelation discloses the existence in man of a higher than moral or voluntary life, a life which has indeed always been symbolized by that, but which puts itself at a hopeless remove from it by rigidly disclaiming a finite genesis, and appealing only to the infinite sanctions. Now science is the organ of the distinctively finite intellect, the intellect tethered to sense; and though doubtless it will one day yield a prompt reverberation, a cordial flooring and support, to the instincts of this higher life, the two spheres are nevertheless as essentially distinct as those of freedom and bondage. (H. James 1869, 67)

Henry's experience of God no longer demands artistic and scientific actualization. Consciousness and interaction marked an important phase in his theory, but revelation, a more passive trust in others, is a higher stage. It enables relationships to develop on principles which are not paternal and benevolent but interactional and equal.

The theory Henry developed had clarified the confusion that had accompanied his unhappy childhood. First he separated moral life from natural life, a process necessitated by his physical injury. Later these were distinguished from spiritual life, moral life having involved the severe emotional pain of abandonment by his father.

Each step along the way of Henry's developing faith established some form of connection between himself and a vision of God. His unshakable faith in God's existence contrasted to his experience of his own vulnerability and confusion. His image of the creator developed through his idealizing fantasy about his father. As he would explore his idealized images of himself and others, he would invariably find himself disappointed: in his own moral limitation, in the church, in art, in science, and finally in relationships.

The disappointments led him to examine his despair and vulnerability and to develop a truer sense of himself and his relationships. Man can never be the creator, he concludes. He must allow himself to experience God through passive revelation rather than active rationalization. His theory has come full circle, returning the process of idealization to one of contemplation rather than action. The circle of his caring has broadened, however. Its focus is relationships rather than the self.

> In a word, God is a *creator*, who gives subjective or conscious life to the work of his hands; while man is at most a *maker*, who gives mere objective or unconscious existence to the conceptions of his genius. Let us beware, then, of reflectively picturing the creative procedure, in giving us selfhood or identity, as by any means an outward, personal, or moral act. (H. James 1869, 114)

Henry's theory provided a format in which he could experience his vulnerability, but in an abstracted manner. His sponsoring activities with his children provided a complementary format in which he protected himself from abandonment by demanding an intense closeness while also developing the security necessary to resolve his feelings toward his father.

Henry found a "great purgative and redemptive process" (H. James 1869, 133) in his capacity to accept the importance of his children. He discusses the relationship between man's alienation and the redemptive love of the creator in a manner which reflects this resolution:

> Redemption shows us the creator joyfully acquiescing in that event, or invisibly accompanying him into the most intimate fastnesses of his alienation, in order *there* to bring about his spiritual or objective restoration. (H. James 1869, 133)

Creative love is more than spontaneity. God reaches out to what is opposite to Himself, accepting the limitations of relationships and transforming this first into alienation and then into true intimacy.

According to Henry, man must undergo a series of painful realizations in order to experience the creative love within him. Early in life he experiences a natural sense of physical independence. Morality initially supports this sense, providing the person with the belief that he is emotionally self-sufficient. The religious sense of moral insufficiency, however, overpowers this pride and leaves man destitute. Only then does man seek relationships in order to give rather than merely to enhance himself. In this way he finds his own creative love. What was initially experienced as an empty, meaningless pain has become the larger shape of creation itself.

Only in acknowledging his selfhood to be a mirror image, a mere shadow of reality, can man sense the deeper forces of community within him. Psychologically one sees in this concept Henry's final turning away from his self-idealizations. He replaces them with an idealized notion of his relationships with his children. He has found that underneath his vulnerability lies a sense of interpersonal connectedness which is more than illusory theory.

Conscience leads men to turn to each other for support. It is "the true point of indifference, indistinction, or identification between man and man" (H. James 1869, 164). In Henry's case it is the saving capacity to turn to relationships to find a security which he could not experience by isolation and self-idealization.

Henry describes this transformation most eloquently as he explains his view of the creator. Love, he argues, must be seen as emptying out of the idealized, distant, essential self into the giving, acting, existential self. It is the principle of life within:

> We suppose him to be somehow *essentially* a creator, whereas he is only *existentially* so; i.e., he creates only in so far as he objectively exists, or goes forth from himself, from his own subjectivity, from his barren and bleak infinitude, and takes up his abode in the finite, or what is not himself, in what indeed from the nature of the case must logically be the exact and total opposite of himself. (H. James 1869, 185)

The activities which involved Henry in relationships with others, particularly his family, led him to focus more fully on the importance of love in his later works. In *Society the Redeemed Form of Man* (1879), his last published work, Henry synthesized this with autobiographical material and expanded his ideas about revelation and love.

Henry distinguishes between two forms of consciousness: scientific, "the deceased or reflective consciousness . . . an essentially servile sphere of the mind"; and religious, "vital and associated consciousness" (H. James 1879, 116). Science has its role in the theory of knowledge and understanding, but it is secondary to revelation. It cannot answer questions of existence but can only serve as a means of developing efficient methods once revelation has taken place. This clarifies Henry's new understanding of the role of love.

In his early writing, scientific progress and action were seen as crucial to human experience. In Henry's later thinking neither science nor art functions as an ideal answer to the problem of meaning in life. If art idealized spontaneity, and science idealized rational action, both are now subordinate to communication: "It is this infinite communication which alone makes created life or consciousness conceivable" (H. James 1879, 261).

This communication is not rational and external but subjective and deeply spiritual. It is not between two objectively existing persons, but it is a sense of union with one's existential reality.

> I for my part will cherish the name of Him alone whose insufficiency to Himself is so abject that He is incapable *of realizing Himself except in others*. (H. James 1879, 334)

Relationships provide Henry with an alternative to idealizing the invulnerable self by actualizing the experience of vulnerability and pain:

> All His infinitude or freedom is mortgaged to the necessity of bringing His creature to ripe natural or spontaneous manhood, and only when that burden is accomplished and that most Divine pleasure realized will He enjoy His first faint chance of seeing *Himself* reflected — *in that happiness of His creation*. (H. James 1879, 460)

Relationships in the abstract provided Henry with a conceptual framework in which he could accept his vulnerability. It was his particular relationship with William, however, in which he hoped to find a solution to his personal limitations. William, the oldest child, had been named after Henry, Sr.'s, father, with whom Henry, Sr., had unsuccessfully sought an ongoing closeness. Temperamental similarities also linked William and Henry, Sr. Both were dramatic, active, and socially outgoing, relying on a combination of judgmental assertiveness and humor. The more challenging style that they shared led to a tendency to use debate and conflict as a primary means of communication. This seems to have met Henry, Sr.'s, long-standing need for someone who could share his optimism without denying contradiction. In this way William could serve as a replacement for William of Albany.

4

Resolving the Philosophical Conflict between William and Henry

Science and Philosophy

William left for Harvard in the fall of 1861. He was 19. Having renounced art as a potential career, he followed his father's wishes by attending the Lawrence Scientific School.

Despite Henry's strong feelings in favor of science, William's scientific background had suffered from the unstructured years of travel and the large number of schools and tutors to which he had been exposed. Science had largely offered him an opportunity to experiment on himself and his brothers. His interests included photography, chemistry, electricity, and marine biology. He was also

> addicted to "experiments" and the consumption of chemicals, . . . the administration to all he could persuade of electric shocks. . . . Then there had been also . . . the finely speculative and boldly disinterested absorption of curious drugs. (H. James, Jr. [1914] 1956, 308)

Scientific experimentation of this sort was far from the study and discipline required in an academic environment. Charles Eliot, his chemistry teacher, later described him as having been easily distracted from the systematic aspects of his work.

William's letters at this time have an intense expressiveness from which one can infer his boredom with traditional academic routine. (For an analysis of this period in William's life which attributes his conflicts to disinterest in science and a continued wish to study art, see Feinstein [1984] and Bjork [1983].)

The letters suggest his longing for excitement and drama. He wrote to his cousin Kitty that as he was reading her letter to him

> a vast crowd collected. Profs. Agassiz and Wyman ran with their notebooks and proceeded to take observations of the greatest import. . . . Up came the fire engines, but I proudly waved them aside and plunged bareheaded into the chill and gloomy bowels of the night, to recover by violent exercise the use of my reasoning faculties, which had almost been annihilated by the shock of happiness. (W. James 1920, I:37)

Of his studies, William wrote to another friend that "relentless chemistry claims its hapless victim" (W. James 1920, I:40), describing in lurid, exaggerated detail how he was subjected to the heat and gases at the chemistry laboratory. His parents learned his plans for his future:

> one year study chemistry, then spend one term at home, then one year with Wyman, then a medical education, then five or six years with Agassiz, then probably death, death, death with inflation and plethora of knowledge. . . . This you had better seriously consider. . . . Your beautiful,
>
> Your Blossom!!
> (W. James 1920, I:42)

In his second year at the Scientific School, William's complaints about the work gave way to anxieties about his future. He was drawn to natural science, but felt that it would be more prudent for him to study medicine. When he finally did decide to enter the Medical School, he did so with many doubts about the effectiveness of doctors. His studies in the Medical School continued to be with Jeffries Wyman, indicating his continued interest in natural science rather than medical practice.

In March 1865, William joined an expedition to Brazil directed by Louis Agassiz, a leading scientist at Harvard. Agassiz hoped to collect evidence in the Amazon which would refute Darwin's theory of evolution. He decided to take several unpaid assistants, and William and his close friend Tom Ward both arranged to go. The trip convinced William that he was not interested in becoming a naturalist, although he enjoyed the experience of traveling in South America. He returned to Boston in March 1866 and spent the summer as an undergraduate intern at Massachusetts General Hospital, living at home. In the fall he resumed his medical studies, but by the winter he had begun to have backaches. In December he wrote to his sister of the process of seeking hospital work in a cynical tone, suggesting his frustration with medical school.

> The present time is a very exciting one for ambitious young men at the Medical School who are anxious to get into the hospital. Their toadying the physicians, asking them intelligent questions after lectures, offering to run errands for them, etc., this week reaches its climax; they call at their residences and humbly solicit them to favor their appointment, and do the same at the residences of the ten trustees. So I have sixteen visits to make. I have little fears, with my talent for flattery and fawning, of a failure. (Perry 1935, I:231)

His back had begun to bother him in November and did not improve. If he received an appointment he did not utilize it. In April 1867 he left for a convalescent trip to Europe. Following a spring and summer in Dresden with little improvement, he went to the baths at Teplitz and then to Berlin. Although he began to feel better, he reported in a letter written in September to Tom Ward that: "medicine is busted—much to my sorrow, for I was beginning to get much attached to it" (Perry 1935, I:244).

During his years as a student at Harvard, William had read widely in the fields of history, literature, and philosophy as well as science. His reading continued during his travels, and his interests in philosophy and science stimulated a debate with his father. According to Perry, it was William's "predestined mission to find a philosophical truth that should justify religion without alienating science" (Perry 1935, I:230). William was predestined in a sense by his father's failure to include the sensory world in his integration of science and religion. William understood his father's failure, and their close philosophical and personal relationship stimulated him to find a resolution.

As a sponsor to William's intellectual life, Henry was both a blessing and a curse. William could see his father's failure and understand its personal components. He could surpass his father in his objective understanding of Henry's philosophy. However, he could not convince his father of its limitations. It was during the years of ill health and depression, from 1866 to 1872, that he worked to define a philosophical world which would include his father's acceptable ideas, and replace those which were more suited for his father than for him.

From Berlin, William began to confront his father with objections to Henry's philosophy. In Teplitz he had received a copy of an article Henry had written for the *North American Review*, "Swedenborg's Ontology" (1867). In his response to this he revealed to his father for the first time the full extent of his unhappiness:

> My confinement to my room and inability to indulge in any social intercourse drove me necessarily into reading a great deal, which in my half-starved and weak condition was very bad for me, making me irritable and tremulous in a way I have never before experienced.... Although I cannot exactly say that I got low-spirited, yet thoughts of the pistol, the dagger and the bowl began to usurp an unduly large part of my attention, and I began to think that some change, even if a hazardous one, was necessary. (W. James 1920, I:95–96)

William's separation from the family and his physical problems forced him to deal with his feelings on his own. He told no one about his anxieties until they assumed the frightening form of intrusive suicidal fantasies. Still William would not admit that he was seriously depressed, at least not to his father. Rather than describe his loneliness and fear or discuss his uncertainties about his future, he engaged his father in a philosophical debate.

William used his relationship with his father to express his need to master his frustration. The supposedly "delightful" backaches which made his brother, Henry, Jr., so "interesting" made him angry and sullen (Perry 1935, I:244). He felt cut off from the world of activity and from the medical career for which he had long prepared. This increased his anxieties and his sense of powerlessness. His doctor advised therapeutic baths. William's reaction was typical of his character:

> While there, owing to the weakening effects of the baths, both back and stomach got worse, if anything; but the beautiful country and a number of drives which I thought myself justified in taking made me as happy as a king. (W. James 1920, I:96)

Activity and exposure to the world rather than rest and isolation were what William needed.

William similarly turned to his father not for consolation but for stimulation and confrontation. He sought a way to communicate his ideas and to share the view of the world he was beginning to define:

> I have read your article, which I got in Teplitz, several times carefully. I must confess that the darkness which to me has always hung over what you have written on these subjects is hardly at all cleared up. Every sentence seems written from a point of view which I nowhere get within range of, and on the other hand ignores all sorts of questions which are visible from my present view. . . . I can understand now no more than ever the world-wide gulf you put between "Head" and "Heart"; to me they are inextricably entangled together, and seem to grow from a common stem — and *no* theory of creation seems to me to make things clearer. I cannot logically understand *your* theory . . . it seems to me the creation is the very arbitrary one you inveigh against; and the whole process is a mere circle of the creator described within his own being and returning to the starting-point. (W. James 1920, I:96–97)

William criticized his father on two major points: the separation of thought and feeling, or of scientific knowledge and spiritual knowledge; and the absence of a clear differentiation of the creator from the creation. The first point is essentially a defense of scientific fact. If there is no separation of head and heart, there is no reason to turn away from the physical world as fragmentary and alienating and toward introspection as a reassuring alternative. The second point captures a logical problem in Henry's theology and a psychological dilemma in his relationship with William.

Henry's idealistic conception of God filled an emptiness in his life and closed off his fears of loneliness and death. In challenging his father's religious philosophy as ignoring the true identity of the physical world, William performed the function which Henry could not undertake. He wished to raise the level of direct physical experience from the phenomenal to the real. This meant that Henry needed to acknowledge his physical separateness as well as his sense of spiritual community.

In essence William interpreted to his father that Henry was afraid to separate himself from his own creation, his family, and that therefore he was intrusive and domineering, despite his tenderness. Henry's behavior, like his philosophy, was "a mere circle of the creator described within his own being and returning to the starting-point" (W. James 1920, I:97). William was not convinced that the creator could actually descend into nature, and that God could thus become his creation. This "seems to be the kernel of the whole" (W. James 1920, I:97).

In fact there is no active role for the creator if one does not separate the head from the heart. For Henry, the creator was an ideal, a concept which provided a guarantee of security and protection. Once anxiety had overwhelmed Henry's sense of intellectual control, the creator played an important function by returning order to the universe. When he could no longer trust his own intentions because circumstances were overwhelming, Henry placed himself in God's hands. The feeling of power that arose when he accepted such an ideal, however, could become destructive, as it threatened to do in his relationship with William.

Henry the philosopher could not pass his ideas along to William without including his experience of the sensory world as fragmentary and anxiety producing. However, Henry as a father had protected William from a direct experience of his deepest anxieties, which had arisen from his father's disinterest. William was forced to come to terms with the blessing of his father's protectiveness and the curse of what had motivated him, Henry's fear of William of Albany's moral condemnation.

William's next letter to his father confronted what he feared would be his father's increased sense of isolation as he learned of William's inability to become his philosophical heir. William seemed to feel that he was walking an emotional tightrope. He did not want to become one of the dangerous and immoral strangers against whom his father had warned him, nor did he wish to mislead his father about his unwillingness to participate in Henry's isolation.

> I want you to feel how thorough is my personal sympathy with you, and how great is my delight in much that I do understand of what you think, and my admiration of it. You live in such mental isolation that I cannot help often feeling bitterly at the thought that you must see in even your own children strangers to what you consider the best part of yourself. But it is a matter in which one's wishes are of little influence, and until something better comes, you can feel sure of the fullest and heartiest *respect* I feel for any living person. (Perry 1935, II:706–7)

William had joined his generation and his larger social world by accepting science as a measure of external reality, not a tool of introspection. He showed naive faith that his challenges would receive a fair appraisal from his father and would elicit some self-examination. However their effect was the opposite. Far from feeling isolated and depressed about himself, Henry responded with typical parental anxiety about the unhappy state of his son's feelings. He defended his ideas as something William was unable to understand because he was too immersed in science:

> I have no great conceit of my expository ability . . . but at the same time it is very evident to me that your trouble in understanding it arises *mainly* from the purely scientific cast of your thought just at present, and the temporary blight exerted thence upon your metaphysic wit. Ontological problems seem very idle to the ordinary scientific imagination, because it is stupefied by the giant superstition we call Nature. (Perry 1935, II:707)

For Henry philosophy required that one turn away from the natural world and reflect on its limitations. The freedom of spiritual introspection was further advanced by the choice of faith in one's true spiritual identity and rejection of the phenomenal, or shadow-like, sense of self.

As Henry developed his argument he moved away from its cultural and social determinants, the critique of pure scientific knowledge, and moved toward its psychological meaning. His focus is already familiar to the reader. He defended the principle of his introspective identity, which he believed William had challenged.

> To argue, then, as you do, that this objective tendency in us is unreal because it has only a subjective provocation or base, is like arguing down my spiritual manhood, my practical objective sympathy with all goodness and truth, because you can scientifically relegate me in all material regards back to animal, vegetable and mineral antecedents. I have the inexpugnable testimony of consciousness to my spiritual reality, a testimony which laughs at all adverse reasoning — which thrives in fact by all outward gainsaying, and only dwindles in an atmosphere of outward concession or acknowledgement. (Perry 1935, II:709)

The threat to Henry's individuality, mastery, and masculinity was William's denial of an ideal principle and his rejection of the self-preserving separation of physical from spiritual experience.

Henry recognized the impoverished quality which spiritual experience suggested when it was cut off from nature. However, he believed that the needs of this isolated spirit could be met by God's presence:

> But how shall the creature command the resources necessary for this end? He is in himself absolutely without funds, being as yet utterly unconscious or non-existent, so that unless his creator is rich and gracious enough to make him a loan, by making over

his existence to him as it were, or allowing him to appropriate it freely as if it were his own, he will never be able to bring himself up to the required level. (Perry 1935, II:710)

By accepting the presence of God one could be rescued from the isolation that initially accompanied the insight that the self was unreal. With faith man could then integrate natural experience as essentially symbolic:

Thus Nature is only a creative form, ceremony, or ritual. It is a living symbol or consecration of the spiritual marriage which is forever going on or deepening between creator and creature; and is *utterly devoid of life but in that aspect.* (Perry 1935, II:710)

Henry's vision of the relationship between creator and creature as a marriage pointed to the intensity of his identification with William. The "loan" which the creator makes to the creature seems to suggest eventual independence for man. As William pointed out, however, Henry's theology began and ended with God. There was no place for an independent process in Henry's world.

This is a contradiction that Henry could not face. He believed that endowing the creature with the experience of alienation granted him true separateness. Similarly he believed that by criticizing William's ideas as inferior to *his* spiritual insights he was helping him to achieve a sense of identity:

I am sure I have something better to tell you than you will be able to learn from all Germany—at least all scientific Germany. So urge me hard to your own profit. Let it go at present into your memory—if not further—that in the true order of thought individuality is primary, and universality or community altogether derivative; that is, that the only universal existence is individual existence. (Perry 1935, II:711)

William's response to his father reiterated and strengthened his earlier points, reflecting increasing confidence in his perceptions. He continued to believe that Henry's view of the creation denied any separate identity for the creature. William argued that man's freedom did not rest in his denial of the physical world but in the possibilities that the world offered. Knowledge was limited to an understanding of the world. The variety of possible interpretations of experience meant that it was impossible to be certain of God's methods and intentions. For man to posit that he knows what they are "means transcending the limits of his creature-ship" (Perry 1935, II:712).

William challenged the spiritual focus of his father and particularly Henry's confidence that he had found the theoretical key to mankind's salvation. His ideas did not promote individuality but idealistic monism. Henry's creator had gone beyond making a loan of some aspect of his identity. "He, in the last resort, bears the whole expense of the operation" (Perry 1935, II:713). Henry's creator was too involved in creation for William's tastes. Henry had rejected his sense of a separate identity, replacing it with a sense of oneness with God. William, being much less afraid of the dangerous consequences of selfhood, preferred to hold on to his separateness. Although he appears to have been anxious about being rejected by his father, judging from his ill health and his physical distance when he confronted Henry, he certainly never faced the moral condemnation which his father had encountered from William of Albany. Henry's fatherly concern had created an experiential and philosophical conflict between his and William's views of the world.

William began to view his father's philosophy as personally meaningful but not necessarily true. He dismissed it from the realm of scientific explanation. This allowed him to accept the ideas as one possible explanation of the universe rather than as the only acceptable alternative.

> Your analysis or Swedenborg's of creation into its elements seems to me a most full and beautiful one, and I do not now think that my possible joy in going forth to meet the Creator in the sort of marriage or equation you represent ought to be diminished by my believing that the thing was after all a piece of "magic" on his part. I cannot attain to any such "inexpugnable testimony of consciousness to my spiritual reality" as that you speak of, and that must be a decisive moment in determining one's attitude toward such problems. *Practically*, it seems to me that *all* tendencies must nowadays unite in philanthropy; perhaps an atheistic tendency more than any, for sympathy is now so much developed in the human breast that misery and undeveloped-ness would all the more powerfully call for correction when coupled with the thought that from nowhere else than from us could correction possibly come—that we ourselves must be our own providence. (Perry 1935, II:714)

In these lines were the seeds of William's pragmatism and radical empiricism. He accepted his father's ideas as empirically meaningful without feeling that they were ontologically valid. He identified his own sympathies as more straightforwardly pluralistic and pragmatic, arguing that taking moral responsibility for the active correction of problems was more important than spiritual insight.

Although this letter concluded William's debate with his father it did not resolve his anxieties. He began to view his own life in terms of his capacity for "simple, patient, monotonous scientific labor day after day" (W. James 1920, I:119). He became critical of his education: "Too late! too late! If I had been *drilled* further in mathematics, physics, chemistry, logic, and the history of metaphysics . . ." (W. James 1920, I:119). To a fellow medical student he jokingly proposed a partnership in which he could continue his medical studies despite his poor health: "you to run around and attend to the patients while I will stay at home and, reading everything imaginable in English, German, and French, distil it in a concentrated form into your mind" (W. James 1920, I:123). The humor was a response to his concerns about finding a career for himself, given his physical problems and his disinterest in the practicalities of being a doctor.

William's close friend and confidant at this time, Tom Ward, wrote to William of feeling depressed. William's response indicated his developing philosophical principles and his divergence from his father's ideas. Primarily he had replaced the idea of God with faith in mankind. Unlike his father, he did not see personal relationships as a means of verifying God's presence. His father's assurance of a socialistic Divine Natural Humanity had been replaced by William's acknowledgment of pain and despair in all human relationships. William believed that we wish for God, for something better than our disappointing experiences, but that responsibility for creating a more positive experience rests with each individual.

> All I can tell you is the thought that with me outlasts all others, and into which, like a rock, I find myself washed up when the waves of doubt are weltering over all the rest of the world; and that is the thought of my having a will, and of my belonging to a brotherhood of men possessed of a capacity for pleasure and pain of different kinds. . . .
>
> I know that in a certain point of view, and the most popular one, this seems a cold activity for our affections, a stone instead of bread. We long for sympathy, for a purely *personal* communication, first with the soul of the world, and then with the soul of our fellows. And happy are they who think, or know, that they have got them! But to those who must confess with bitter anguish that they are perfectly isolated from the soul of the world, and that the closest human love encloses a potential germ of estrangement or hatred, that all *personal* relation is finite, conditional, mixed . . ., it may not prove such an unfruitful substitute. . . . Every thought you now have and every act and intention owes its complexion to the acts of your dead and living brothers. *Everything* we know and are is through men. We have no revelation but through man. . . . However mean a man may be, man is *the best we know*; and your loathing as you turn from what you probably call the vulgarity of human life — your homesick yearning for a *Better*, somewhere — is furnished by your manhood; your ideal is made up of traits suggested by past men's words and actions.
>
> . . . So that it seems to me that a sympathy with men as such and a desire to contribute to the will of a species, which, whatever may be said of it, contains All that we acknowledge as good, may very well form an external interest sufficient to keep one's moral pot boiling in a very lively manner to a good old age. The idea, in short, of becoming an accomplice in a sort of "Mankind its own God or Providence" scheme is a *practical* one.
>
> . . . I confess that, in the lonesome gloom which beset me for a couple of months last summer, the only feeling that kept me from giving up was that by waiting and living, by hook or crook, long enough, I might make my *nick*, however small a one, in the raw stuff the race has got to shape, and so assert my reality. (W. James 1920, I:130–32)

To the reader familiar with William's philosophy, these passages sound familiar. His future intellectual work consisted of first constructing a theory of psychology that supported his point of view and then articulating in a philosophical context his crucial beliefs in the importance of activity and human relationships.

At the end of the month in which he wrote this letter, January 1868, William returned to the baths at Teplitz. He wrote to his father that his return marked not a worsening of his condition but an eagerness to improve more quickly. He had begun to think of a career studying and teaching physiology.

Accepting a Scientific Universe

The baths did not improve William's backaches nor did a summer trip to Divonne, where he undertook another water cure. William therefore decided to leave Europe and return home to Cambridge. There he finished his medical degree in June 1869, read voraciously, and sank again into a deep depression.

After his debate with his father William had become much more comfortable about pursuing a scientific career. He called it "my only ideal in life" in a letter to Tom Ward written in December 1868 (Perry 1935, I:287). After six months of preparation for his degree, however, he no longer felt able to trust his strength. He wrote to Henry, Jr., who was taking his convalescent trip to Europe:

> I wrote to you that my bottom rather fell out two and a half months ago. I've not picked up since.... This summer with *no* study and hardly any reading may start me up again. If not, I genuinely don't much care, for I have loosed the lock-jaw grasp with which I clung to the hope of accomplishing external work, and transferred my interest in the game of life to the subjective attitude, *i.e.*, become moralized, in some sort. (Perry 1935, I:298)

There can be no question but that William experienced the prospective loss of a scientific career as a bitter disappointment despite his attempt to "become moralized" and adjust to it. He and his family traveled to Promfret for a restful summer. William, feeling empty about losing science and reluctant to overstimulate himself, began to study psychology. His conflict about his health and his future was reflected in a note he wrote while he was there:

> To "accept the universe," to protest against it, *voluntary* alternatives. So that in a given case of evil the mind seesaws between the effort to improve it away, and resignation. The second not being resorted to till the first has failed, it would seem either that the second were an insincere *pis aller*, or the first a superfluous vanity. The solution can only lie in taking neither absolutely, but in making the resignation only provisional (that is, voluntary, conditional), and the attempt to improve to have its worth in the action rather than the result. Thus resignation affords ground and leisure to advance to new philanthropic action. Resignation should not say, "It is good," "a mild yoke," and so forth, but "I'm willing to stand it for the present." This brings matters back to proposition (a). What the man *wants*, more or less, being the ultimate appeal for him.

Three quantities to determine. (1) how much pain I'll stand; (2) how much other's pain I'll inflict (by existing); (3) how much other's pain I'll "accept," without ceasing to take pleasure in their existence. (Perry 1935, I:301-2)

In his earlier letter to Tom Ward, William had seemed assured that by believing in relationships he might influence the quality of his own and others' lives. His uncertainty about this issue was reflected in this note. To believe he had control over his feelings was, he feared, superfluous vanity. On the other hand, to do nothing and merely resign himself to depression suggested moral weakness. Finally William came to a tentative acceptance of his own unhappiness, with the understanding that this form of acceptance did not preclude some form of action if the unhappiness became overwhelming. William did experience an improvement in his health during the summer followed by a collapse a week before returning to Cambridge.

At the beginning of October William wrote to Henry, Jr., in regard to the publication of their father's book, *The Secret of Swedenborg* (1869):

Suffice it that many points which before were incomprehensible to me because doubtfully fallacious, I now definitely believe to be entirely fallacious; but as this pile accumulates on one side there is left a more and more definite residuum on the other of great and original ideas, so that my respect for him is on the whole increased rather than diminished. But his ignorance of the way of thinking of other men, and his cool neglect of their difficulties, is fabulous in a writer on such subjects. It is pure theology, and not philosophy commonly so-called, that he deals with. (Perry 1935, I:307)

William continued to feel alienated from his father's ideas. His complaint about Henry's "cool neglect" of other men's difficulties suggests no change in Henry's unwillingness to accept science or William's dilemma about his future. That William's invalidism would force him into a speculative life could be no great loss from Henry's point of view. Rather it would fulfill his hopes for a theological heir.

William however continued to maintain a different view of philosophy than did his father, as is reflected in the letter. For William to undertake a speculative life meant not to accept his father's idealism but to develop a theoretical and logical defense of his belief in science, moral choice, and pragmatic action. Two diary entries from the winter of 1870 mark his progress in this struggle. The first suggests his dread of failure and his continuing ambivalence about following his father's example as an introspectionist:

Today I about touched bottom, and perceive plainly that I must face the choice with open eyes: shall I *frankly* throw the moral business overboard, as one unsuited to my innate aptitudes, or shall I follow it, and it alone, making everything else merely stuff for

> it? I will give the latter alternative a fair trial. Who knows but the moral interest may become developed. . . . Hitherto I have tried to fire myself with the moral interest, as an aid in the accomplishing of certain utilitarian ends. (Perry 1935, I:322)

William had begun to consider the possibility of following his father into "the moral business," his father's philosophical career. His uncertainty about whether he might not be suited for it may have been a sign of his fears of publicly challenging his father's certitude about divine control over human experience.

William may also have been involved in an attempt to make himself well by regarding the physical aspects of his problems as psychologically based. He was unwilling to use reassurance as a form of self-cure, having found this to be one of the least palatable aspects of the medical profession. Nevertheless, his pain seems to have been as much interpersonal as physical in nature.

The issue of physical-versus-moral causation of disease would suggest conflicts over introspection versus science. Feinstein (1970) has written an article on the psychological meaning of William's later theory of the emotions arguing that William's resolutions tended to fall into the category of moral and idealistic thought:

> suppression and moral exhortation on the conscious level and repression and denial on the level of unconscious mental functioning. (142)

This conclusion, when viewed in the context of William's family environment, seems more applicable to Henry. William sought to replace these processes with a scientific attitude and did so essentially without the support or understanding of his father. It is possible that he was forced to hold to his scientific views precisely because moral exhortation did not cure his physical symptoms.

Henry had used his theory to mask underlying anxiety. For William, the process of developing his ideas was more painful but more flexible. He experienced the despair underneath his theory of moral action and thus struggled with the feelings of touching bottom and having the bottom drop out, as he described in his diary and his letter to Henry, Jr. These feelings may be contrasted to the more comfortable split which his father had been able to create between his anxieties and his religious beliefs. Henry was able to view his terror as a physical phenomenon not in the same realm of reality as his spiritual confidence. William saw this as an illusion.

Religious Conversion

In rejecting his father's introspectionist theology, William also enabled himself to use his ideas as psychological tools. This can be seen in his reaction to a terrifying image which resembled the one which precipitated his father's religious conversion. William reported the incident in *The Varieties of Religious Experience* ([1902] 1958), attributing it to a Frenchman. Although the date of the incident is not known, his son attributed it to the period of depression in William's young adulthood. William introduced the passage in which he discussed his terror by saying: "The worst kind of melancholy is that which takes the form of panic fear." He continued:

> Whilst in this state of philosophic pessimism and general depression of spirits about my prospects, I went one evening into a dressing-room in the twilight to procure some article that was there; when suddenly there fell upon me without any warning, just as if it came out of the darkness, a horrible fear of my own existence. Simultaneously there arose in my mind the image of an epileptic patient whom I had seen in the asylum, a black-haired youth with greenish skin, entirely idiotic, who used to sit all day on one of the benches, or rather shelves against the wall, with his knees drawn up against his chin, and the coarse gray undershirt, which was his only garment, drawn over them inclosing his entire figure. He sat there like a sort of sculptured Egyptian cat or Peruvian mummy, moving nothing but his black eyes and looking absolutely non-human. This image and my fear entered into a species of combination with each other. *That shape am I*, I felt, potentially. Nothing that I possess can defend me against that fate, if the hour for it should strike for me as it struck for him. There was such a horror of him, and such a perception of my own merely momentary discrepancy from him, that it was as if something hitherto solid within my breast gave way entirely, and I became a mass of quivering fear. After this the universe was changed for me altogether. I awoke morning after morning with a horrible dread at the pit of my stomach, and with a sense of the insecurity of life that I never knew before, and that I have never felt since. (W. James [1902] 1958, 135-36)

While there are many similarities between William's despair and his father's religious conversion, the contrasts are more striking. The entire explanation in fact was defined by contrasts which indicated William's increased receptivity to his anxiety when compared to his father. Henry reported himself as having been unusually optimistic before his religious experience. William was depressed. Henry feared objective evil. William feared his own existence; not the existence of evil but his vulnerability to it. William saw a diseased patient who unlike his father had not compensated intellectually for his physical trauma, while Henry saw an inhuman figure.

Disturbed by his father's insensitivity to him, William had begun to question his father's wisdom and to grasp the terror of Henry's conversion. Losing his image of his father as protective, he experienced something akin to his father's religious fear. The figure which William viewed however was not a fantasy shape, an embodiment of evil, but a real person whose physical disabilities had turned him into a living corpse. This image is of his father as unresponsive and emotionally paralyzed. In order to understand his father, William had to acknowledge Henry's despair, expressed in his denial of physical reality. This contrasted with his father's resolution, which perpetuated his idealization of his father by projecting it into religious thought.

The devil which Henry had seen made it possible for him to believe in spiritual salvation. William, who was focused on his earthly rather than his heavenly father, had begun to view Henry realistically and honestly. This enabled him to accept his own vulnerability and his terror. The vulnerability emerged on an intense level in this experience and led William to renewed attempts to balance his sense of safety and belief.

Not pain but an overwhelming connection terrified William. For Henry an imaginary connection had meant salvation, for it allowed him to actualize his relationship with his father. William found that the connection led to a tragic view of his father and a fear of too much intimacy. His psychological development paralleled his need for a separate personal identity. He began to imagine and experience the terror of becoming too much like his father. A false sense of identity threatened to overwhelm him. "That shape am I, I felt, potentially." This understanding enhanced the process of forming an adult identity not dependent on the intense support system of his family.

To create a monistic system was dangerous in William's view. Henry had religiously adhered to one system, never questioning it despite the lack of response from others. William's imagery suggests that this rigidity reflected his father's pain and his unacknowledged disappointment in William of Albany. William's ability to acknowledge himself as "potentially" vulnerable clarified his terror of having a close relationship with his father. Even to imagine himself as a victim filled him with "the insecurity of life that I never knew before."

William needed to find some indication of true autonomy. The passivity symbolized by the epileptic suggests that William's relationship with his father carried with it the danger of a paralyzed dependency. His solution to the problem of relating to his father involved an acceptance of both his vulnerability and a set of active principles. This prevented him from allowing the tragic aspects of his father's experience to mask the conflict between them.

Since William included his description of his religious experience in a chapter on "The Sick Soul" in *The Varieties of Religious Experience*, one expects some form of conversion or resolution to follow. In the following letter to Tom Ward of March 1869, there is again reference to touching bottom. In this case however there was a sense of increasing control.

William adopted empiricism, which now surrounded him as he had once complained of being surrounded by idealism:

> there is an inextinguishable spark which will, when we least expect it, flash out and reveal the existence, at least, of something real—of reason at the bottom of things. . . . I feel that we are Nature through and through, that we are wholly conditioned, that not a wiggle of our will happens save as the result of physical laws; and yet, notwithstanding, we are *en rapport* with reason . . . (W. James 1920, I:152-53)

The empiricism and materialism that William accepted were equivalent to his acceptance of his own terror. They threatened to overpower him, to stamp out reason and individuality. His father's philosophy had been based on this supposition. However William found that when he accepted empirical reality, reason remained. He accepted the terror of his religious experience and his father's vulnerability without finding that it forced a conversion to idealism onto him. In fact the acceptance and acknowledgment of his anxiety freed him to pursue his own philosophical interest in science and empirical evidence.

However, the new pursuit threatened his individuality. His father was not entirely wrong in this regard, to the extent that science justified a materialistic and mechanistic flight from psychological experience. William found the empirical doctrine of psychological determinism unacceptable. Although he embraced the physical world as the only true world and its laws as valid, he refused to believe that reason played no part in experience. This led to a split in William's thought (between mental experience and physical laws) which was finally repaired in his philosophy. William felt he had to accept both, although he was unclear as to how he might fit them together.

William's theoretical uncertainty made it difficult for him to accept the validity of belief until he found validation for it in the writings of the French philosopher Charles Renouvier. On April 30, 1870, he wrote in his diary:

> I think yesterday was a crisis in my life. I finished the first part of Renouvier's second "Essais" and see no reason why his definition of Free Will—"the sustaining of a thought *because I choose to* when I might have other thoughts"—need be the definition of an illusion. . . . My first act of free will shall be to believe in free will. . . . Hitherto, when I have felt like taking a free initiative, like daring to act originally, without carefully waiting for contemplation of the external world to determine all for me, suicide seemed the most manly form to put my daring into; now, I will go a step further with my will; not only act with it, but believe as well; believe in my individual reality and creative power. My belief, to be sure, *can't* be optimistic—but I will posit life (the real, the good) in the self-governing *resistance* of the ego to the world. (W. James 1920, I:147-48)

After this entry there is no information on William's psychological status until August 1872, when he was appointed to a position as instructor of physiology at Harvard. He described the work as "a perfect God-send" (W. James 1920, I:167) in a letter to Henry, Jr. At this point the resolution had its desired effect and he found himself able to withstand the pressures of the academic work.

There was a brief period of ill health following the completion of his first year of teaching during which William traveled again to Europe for a few months. Two documents from that spring provide a final glimpse of William's ambivalence about his career. His son, Henry James III, later wrote:

> These hesitations, and a few months in Europe, marked the end of the period of morbid depression through which the reader has been following him. He returned to America eager for work. (W. James 1920, I:171)

The first document is a letter written by Henry, Sr., to Henry, Jr., commenting on William's improvement. The letter indicates once again Henry's resistance to William's scientific interests. He seemed unaware that William might be finding a satisfaction in teaching because it had filled his need for a scientific profession and had given him an active rather than an introspective role in life. The letter began with a description of William's success as a teacher and his good spirits, in contrast to his former hypochondriacal state. Henry reported that he asked the reasons for the improvement.

> He said . . . more than anything else, his having given up the notion that all mental disorder requires to have a physical basis. This had become perfectly untrue to him. He saw that the mind does act irrespectively of material coercion, and could be dealt with therefore at first hand, and this was health to his bones. It was a splendid declaration, and though I had known from unerring signs of the fact of the change, I had never been more delighted than by hearing of it so unreservedly from his own lips. He has been shaking off his respect for men of mere science as such, and is even more universal and impartial in his judgements than I have known him before. (W James 1920, I:169-70)

William's point of view, confided to his diary, was contrary to that of his father. He rejected the philosophical questioning which he had undergone in his years of poor health and again substituted for it the activities of the man of science.

> Philosophical activity *as a business* is not normal for most men, and not for me. . . . To make the *form* of all possible thought the prevailing *matter* of one's thought breeds hypochondria. Of course my deepest interest will as ever lie with the most general problems. But . . . my strongest moral and intellectual craving is for some stable reality to lean upon. . . . That gets reality for us in which we place our responsibility, and the

concrete facts in which a biologist's responsibilities lie form a fixed basis from which to aspire as much as he pleases to the mastery of universal questions when the gallant mood is on him; and a basis, too, upon which he can passively float and tide over times of weakness and depression, trusting all the while blindly in the beneficence of nature's forces and the return of higher opportunities. (Perry 1935, I:343)

William's Acceptance of Henry's Identity

Henry died in December 1882 at the age of 71. William was in Europe at the time, having arranged with the college to take a year's leave of absence. On learning that his father was seriously ill, he wrote to him in hopes of reaching him before his death:

> All my intellectual life I derive from you; and though we have often seemed at odds in the expression thereof, I'm sure there's a harmony somewhere, and that our strivings will combine. What my debt to you is goes beyond all my power of estimating, — so early, so penetrating and so constant has been the influence. (W. James 1920, I:219)

William also promised his father that he would take care of his literary remains.

In 1884 William published *The Literary Remains of the Late Henry James*. He included his father's unpublished autobiography, portions of an unfinished book, and an introduction. The introduction gave William a further opportunity to clarify the differences between his own and his father's ideas.

William found his father's writings to consist of a rich, well-articulated, and fascinating exposition of ideas which were "singularly unvaried and few" (W. James 1884, 9). He paid tribute to the originality of his father's point of view and to Henry's sense of conviction:

> for he was a religious prophet and genius, if ever prophet and genius there were. He published an intensely positive, radical, and fresh conception of God, and an intensely vital view of our connection with him. (W. James 1884, 12)

For Henry, the traumatic incident of his life had no intentional source. He had not expected nor willed it, nor could he wish it away. He could only respond as fully as his understanding of himself would allow. His experience was so frightfully intense that it required a form of totalistic acceptance, thus shaping a unitary sense of self. His salvation came with a similar experience of inner intensity through his growing capacity to construct idealizations. His theology did not separate this experience into its objective components of himself and others but captured the transcendent quality of relationships. William respected the convictions which his father held. His view of the world, however flawed, gave his children a sense of the importance of ideas and values.

For Henry, man's fundamental error was in viewing shadow as substance, thus appropriating to himself some choice and autonomy which in fact he did not have. His notion of moral development was that it was forced on man because of the pain of experiencing his separate identity. This led Henry to focus on his dependency on God as He was manifested in human community. Religious belief preserved the intensity of the imaginary tie with William of Albany while distancing him from the realities of his father's anger and his own injury.

Henry also used belief to provide the basis for an allegorical and tentative psychology. The realities of relationships and self might be worked out inwardly and philosophically, providing guidelines and explanations for one's actual experiences. Yet one must be cautious always to put the spiritual, or philosophical, dimensions first. Otherwise one risked being overwhelmed by the confusion, diversity, and uncertainty of experience.

From William's more scientific perspective, his father's identity was never truly coherent, because Henry denied the importance of perceptual and sensory experience. William disagreed with this aspect of his father's beliefs on both philosophical and psychological grounds. In doing so he concentrated on separating issues of belief from those of the self. It was by combining these two ideas that Henry had achieved his philosophical system at the expense of accepting any objective basis for reality.

For William, experience, divisive and confusing as it might be, was an essential cornerstone of all belief. He attributed his father's beliefs to Henry's doubts and anxieties. William believed that his father had been unable to cope with the possibility of moral uncertainty. Henry had constructed a monistic system that guaranteed the goodness of God and rejected the reality of evil.

Psychologically, William viewed his father's certainty about salvation as a belief that arose from terror. In Henry's theology man initially constructed an idealized self. When he sensed the failure of this construct, he sought coherence in his view of God and thus was able to derive a sense of identity from a monistic, or deterministic, religious vision. The intensity of Henry's conviction could for him overshadow the unpleasantness of reality. For William, however, it revealed his father's tremendous sensitivity to emotional pain.

> I fancy that his belief in its truth was strongest when the dumb sense of human life, sickened and baffled as it is forever by the strange unnatural fever in its breast of unreality and dearth struggling with infinite fulness and possession, became a sort of voice within him, and cried out, "This *must* stop! The good, the good, is really *there*, and *must* see to its own! Who is its own? Is it this querulous usurping, jealous *me*, sickened of

defeat and done to death, and glad never to raise its head again? Never more! It is some sweeter, larger, more innocent and generous receptacle of life than that cadaverous and lying thing can ever be. Let *that* but be removed, and the other may come in. And there must be a way to remove it, for God himself is there, and cannot be frustrated forever of his aim, — least of all by such an obstacle as that! He must *somehow*, and by eternal necessity he *shall*, bring the kingdom of heaven about!" (W. James 1884, 25)

Turning toward God became a means of securing one's existential reality. If one's self was not good then God must exist, for there must be good somewhere. The goodness of God could guarantee the security of one's identity and a potential community of interpersonal relationships.

Religious conversion provided Henry with a sense of identity. When he tried to "*appropriate* the goodness" of life he sensed his inadequacy. When he naively attempted to attribute immortal identity to himself he discovered his conflictual psychological state. The pain of finding himself so much less than his ideal led him to reject the self and replace it by faith in God's love. By spiritualizing the meaningfulness which he had desired in himself he minimized the unsettling dimensions of inner conflict. Belief had provided an escape from anxiety.

William's account pointed to the renunciation of emotional turmoil which "*must* stop!" and the subsequent embrace of something larger than the inadequate self: "some sweeter, larger, more innocent and generous receptacle of life than that cadaverous and lying thing can ever be." The goodness which life offered could be accepted through an act of transformation and conversion, a sense that it "must come to be, if God truly exists, — an assumption that we *owe* to his power and his love" (W. James 1884, 26).

In his philosophical debates with Henry, William argued that sensory experience was equally as real as inner inspiration. In *The Literary Remains* he carried this critique a step further by suggesting that religious conversion was not a matter of true choice but of a flight from terror. In contrast to his father, William developed a different philosophy. His father's life had represented a longing for a secure understanding of reality. William's philosophy embraced uncertainty and uniqueness. Henry's spiritual world was essentially unitary. William's view of the self was pluralistic. Henry sought truth through introspection, while William turned to the sensory aspects of experience.

William viewed these distinctions as crucial and believed his father to have done so as well:

There is however a pluralism hardened by reflection, and deliberate; a pluralism which, in face of the old mystery of the One and the Many, has vainly sought peace in identification, and ended by taking sides against the One. It seems to me that the deepest of all philosophic differences is that between this pluralism and all forms of monism whatever. Apart from analytic and intellectual arguments, pluralism is a view to which we all practically incline when in the full and successful exercise of our moral energy. The life we then feel tingling through us vouches sufficiently for itself, and nothing tempts us to refer it to a higher source. Being, as we are, a match for whatever evils actually confront us, we rather prefer to think of them as endowed with reality, and as being absolutely alien, but, we hope, subjugable powers. . . . The feeling of *action*, in short, makes us turn a deaf ear to the thought of *being*; and this deafness and insensibility may be said to form an integral part of what in popular phrase is known as "healthy-mindedness." Any absolute moralism must needs be such a healthy-minded pluralism; and in a pluralistic philosophy the healthy-minded moralist will always feel himself at home. (W. James 1884, 116–17)

William had "vainly sought peace in identification" with his father's monistic beliefs and had pulled away from this into the realm of an independent philosophy. In his pluralism life "tingles" through the real body and observable experience, not the ideal spirit. In this world of options the real fears of evil were surmountable by action, not by spiritual imagery.

William's feelings about Henry's theology were ambivalent. On the one hand Henry was a religious genius, while on the other hand he had a morbid and negative view of himself. Henry had constructed an impressive intellectual system, but he could not help his son develop a sense of separateness. This revealed the underlying weakness in Henry's ideas and his relationships. His theology had not helped him with the problem of autonomy, when this meant losing the support of his son.

From William's point of view his father's faith was an admirable attempt to find inner security. However, he realized that he, unlike his father, was basically "healthy-minded" and only potentially disturbed. His healthy-mindedness was a product of his natural sense of separateness rather than the alienation that his father had felt. He continued the passage quoted above in a vein which suggests how deeply empathic he was with the view of reality which he did not share:

But healthy-mindedness is not the whole of life; and the *morbid* view, as one by contrast may call it, asks for a philosophy very different from that of absolute moralism. To suggest personal will and effort to one "all sicklied o'er" with the sense of weakness, of helpless failure, and of fear, is to suggest the most horrible of things to him. What he craves is to be consoled in his very impotence, to feel that the Powers of the Universe recognize and secure him, all passive and failing as he is. Well, we are all *potentially* such sick men. The sanest and best of us are of one clay with lunatics and prison-inmates. And whenever we feel this, such a sense of the vanity of our morality appears but as a plaster hiding a sore it can never cure, and all our well-doing as the hollowest substitute for that well-*being* that our lives ought to be grounded in, but, alas! are not. (W. James 1884, 117–18)

In this way William clarified the reasons for which he turned away from his father's ideas. He sensed their attraction and had also experienced the pain and personal insecurity which underlay their power. But he separated his own healthy contradictory view of reality from the seductive purity of his father's theology. He rejected the implicit invitation of identifying with the weakness which his father had revealed. He experienced his anxiety and limitations as a means of accepting the possibility of moral action, pluralism, and personal autonomy.

This enabled William to defend the validity of his father's ideas on scientific and rational grounds without accepting them as his own. Henry had forced William's hand in this process. He had unintentionally revealed to him the frightening and uninviting dimensions of his identity in his rigid expectations that William's scientific interests would be incorporated into a speculative life. The conflict in their relationship helped William clarify his own healthy-minded separateness.

In his psychology and his philosophy William maintained the separateness of his own identity by focusing on pluralism, pragmatism, and scientific empiricism. He integrated those of his father's ideas which he accepted into his discussions of religious experience, belief, and the continuity and personal meaning of the sense of self.

William's theoretical debt to his father was embedded in more than those ideas which he accepted and rejected. The special father-son relationship remained an important emotional influence throughout his life. The essential separateness of the two men and their two philosophies did not undermine the powerful experience of caring which Henry did successfully convey to his oldest son.

Plate 1. North Pearl Street, Albany, c. 1805–10

Plate 2. North Pearl Street, Albany, as it was in 1814

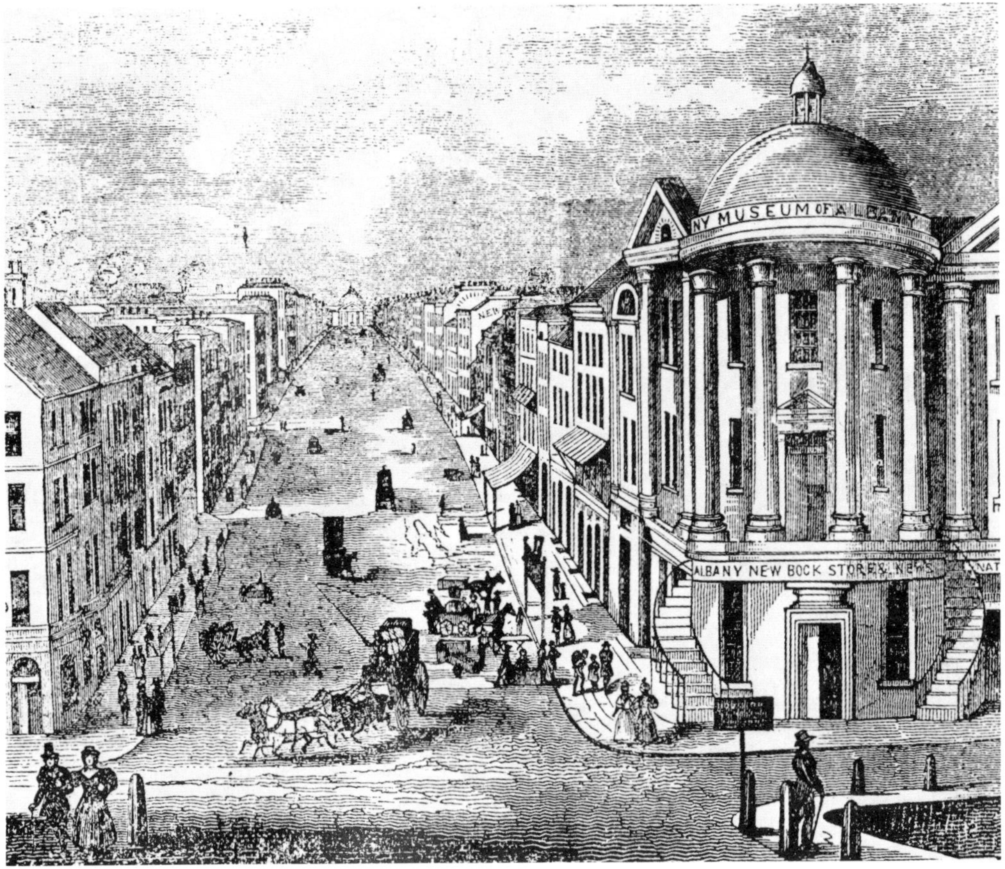

Plate 3. State Street, Albany, 1837

Plate 4. William James of Albany, c. 1810

Plate 5. Henry James, Sr., c. 1873–78

Plate 6. Mary James, c. 1880

Plate 7. William James at 18, c. 1860

Plate 8. William James in Brazil, 1865

Plate 9. William James at about 24, c. 1866

Plate 10. **Pencil sketch** of himself by William James, c. 1866

Plate 11. William James, 1903

Plate 12. Henry James, Jr., and William James, c. 1900

Plate 13. Henry James, Jr., and William James, c. 1905

Plate 14. Alice James, 1870

Plate 15. Robertson James, 1872

Plate 16. Garth Wilkinson James, c. 1873

Bibliography

Barzun, J. 1974. *Clio and the doctors*; *psychohistory, quantohistory, and history*. Chicago: University of Chicago Press.
Bjork, D.W. 1983. *The compromised scientist*: *Wlliam James in the development of American psychology*. New York: Columbia University Press.
Campbell, D.T. 1969. Prospective: Artifact and control. In *Artifact in behavioral research*, ed. R. Rosenthal and R.L. Rosnow. New York: Academic Press.
deMause, L. 1974. The evolution of childhood. In *The history of childhood*, ed. L. deMause. New York: Psychohistory Press.
Demos, J. 1970. *A little commonwealth*: *Family Life in Plymouth Colony*. New York: Oxford University Press.
Erikson, E.H. 1958. *Young man Luther*: *A study in psychoanalysis and history*. New York: Norton.
———. 1963. *Childhood and Society*. Rev. ed. New York: Norton.
———. 1964. *Insight and responsibility:Lectures on the ethical implications of psychoanalytic insight*. New York: Norton.
———. 1969. *Gandhi's truth*: *On the origins of militant nonviolence*. New York: Norton.
———. 1975. *Life history and the historical moment*. New York: Norton.
Erikson, K. T. 1976. *Everything in its path*: *Destruction of community in the Buffalo Creek flood*. New York: Simon and Schuster.
Feinstein, H. M. 1970. William James on the emotions. *Journal of the History of Ideas*, *31*:133-42.
———. 1984. *Becoming William James*. Ithaca: Cornell University Press.
Freud, S. [1928] 1963. Dostoevsky and parricide. In *Character and Culture*, ed. P. Rieff, trans. J. Strachey. New York: Macmillan.
Gedo, J., and Goldberg, A. 1973. *Models of the mind*: *A psychoanalytic theory*. Chicago: University of Chicago Press.
Grattan, C. H. 1932. *The three Jameses*: *A family of minds*. London: Longmans, Green.
Hartmann, H. [1939] 1958. *Ego psychology and the problem of adaptation*, trans. D. Rapaport. New York: International Universities Press.
Hislop, C. 1971. *Eliphalet Nott*. Middletown, Connecticut: Wesleyan University Press.
Hunt, D. 1970. *Parents and children in history:The psychology of family life in early modern France*. New York: Basic Books.
Jacobson, E. 1964. *The self and the object world*. New York: International Universities Press.
James, A. 1965. *The diary of Alice James*, ed. L. Edel. London: Rupert Hart-Davis.
James, H., Sr. 1846. *What constitutes the state*. New York: John Allen.
———. 1850. *Moralism and Christianity*: *Or man's experience and destiny*. New York: Redfield.

———. 1852. *Lectures and miscellanies.* New York: Redfield.

———. 1855. *The nature of evil, considered in a letter to the Rev. Edward Beecher, D.D., author of 'The conflict of ages.'* New York: Appleton.

———. 1857. *Christianity the logic of creation.* New York: Appleton.

———. 1863. *Substance and shadow: Or, morality and religion in their relation to life: An essay on the physics of creation.* Boston: Ticknor and Fields.

———. 1869. *The secret of Swedenborg: Being an elucidation of his doctrine of the Divine Natural Humanity.* Boston: Fields, Osgood.

———. 1875. The woman thou gavest me. *The Atlantic Monthly,* 25, 66–72. (a)

———. 1875. Is marriage holy? *The Atlantic Monthly,* 25, 360–68. (b)

———. 1881. Some personal recollections of Carlyle. *The Atlantic Monthly,* 47:593–609.

———. 1879. *Society the redeemed form of man, and the earnest of God's omnipotence in human nature: Affirmed in letters to a friend.* Boston: Houghton, Osgood.

James, H., Jr. [1913] 1956. A small boy and others. In *Henry James: Autobiography,* ed. F. W. Dupee. New York: Criterion Books.

———.[1914] 1956. Notes of a son and brother. In *Henry James: Autobiography,* ed. F. W. Dupee. New York: Criterion Books.

James, W. 1884. *The literary remains of the late Henry James.* Boston: Houghton Mifflin.

———.[1902] 1958. *The varieties of religious experience.* New York: New American Library.

———. 1920. *The letters of William James* (Vol. I), ed. H. James, III. Boston: Atlantic Monthly Press.

Janik, A., and Toulmin, S. 1973. *Wittgenstein's Vienna.* New York: Simon and Schuster.

LeClair, R. C. 1955. *Young Henry James: 1843–1870.* New York: Twayne Publishers.

Lifton, R. J. [1965] 1970. Psychoanalysis and history. In *History and human survival; essays on the young and old, survivors and the dead, peace and war, and on contemporary psychohistory.* New York: Random House.

———. 1974. On psychohistory. In *Explorations in psychohistory,* ed. R. J. Lifton. New York: Simon and Schuster.

Mazlish, B. 1975. *James and John Stuart Mill: Father and son in the nineteenth century.* New York: Basic Books.

Munsell, J. 1869. *The annals of Albany,* vol. 1. Albany: Joel Munsell.

Perry, R. B. 1935. *The thought and character of William James: As revealed in unpublished correspondence and notes, together with his published writings,* 2 vols. Boston: Little, Brown.

Rapaport, D. A. [1958] 1967. Historical survey of psychoanalytic ego psychology. In *The collected papers of David Rapaport,* ed. M.M. Gill. New York: Basic Books.

———.[1966] 1967. Dynamic psychology and Kantian epistemology. In *The collected papers of David Rapaport,* ed. M.M. Gill. New York: Basic Books.

———.[1954] 1967. Clinical implications of ego psychology. In *The collected papers of David Rapaport,* ed. M.M. Gill. New York: Basic Books.

———.[1956] 1967. Present-day ego psychology. In *The collected papers of David Rapaport,* ed. M.M. Gill. New York: Basic Books.

Rosenzweig, S. 1943. The ghost of Henry James: A study in thematic apperception. *Character and Personality,* 13:79–100.

Schaefer, R. 1968. *Aspects of internalization.* New York: International Universities Press.

Strouse, J. 1980. *Alice James, a biography.* Boston: Houghton Mifflin.

Strout, C. 1968. William James and the twice-born sick soul. *Daedalus,* 97:1062–82.

Warren, A. 1934. *The elder Henry James.* New York: Macmillan.

Weise, A. J. 1884. *The history of the city of Albany, New York from the discovery of the great river in 1524, by Verrazzano, to the present time.* Albany: E. H. Bender.

Young, F. H. 1951. *The philosophy of Henry James, Sr.* New York: Bookman.

Index

Page numbers for illustrations are in italics

Action, 51, 56, 73; Henry James, Sr.'s theory of spontaneous action, 51-52
Agassiz, Louis, 64
Albany, 13, *85, 87, 89*
Alienation, 50, 58
Atlantic, 32

Calvinism, 16, 29, 32
Carlyle, Thomas, 32-34, 35
Childhood and Society (E. H. Erikson), 6
Church of Christ Not an Ecclesiasticism, A Letter to a Sectarian, The (Henry James, Sr.), 41
Conscience, 55, 61. See also Moral development, Morality
Consciousness, Henry James, Sr.'s definition of, 56-59; scientific vs. religious, 61
Creation (by God), 55-56, 58-60

Daily Albany Arbus, 27
Daily Craftsman (Albany), 27
Daily Tribune (New York), 42
de Mause, L., 5
Demos, J., 5
Dynamic psychology, 3, 4

Ego psychology, 4, 5, 6
Eliot, Charles, 63
Emerson, Ralph Waldo, 30-31, 34, 35, 36, 37, 38, 40, 41
Emotional illness, health in the James family, 44
Erikson, E. H., 1, 4, 6; *Childhood and Society,* 6; psychohistorical theory, 3-12; *Young Man Luther,* 7
Erikson, Kai, 4

Faraday, Michael, 29
Feinstein, H. M., 74
Fourier, François, 37
Fraternity, first, in America, 23
Freud, Sigmund, 6

Gedo, J., and A. Goldberg, 5
Glasite movement, 29
Godwin, Parke, 37

Harbinger (journal), 37
Hartmann, H., 4
Harvard University, 63, 78
Henry, Joseph, 22, 28, 29, 31, 48
Historical actuality, 6, 11
Hodge, Dr. Charles, 28
Hunt, D., 5

Identity, 1, 5, 6-9, 15, 24, 34, 35, 36, 50, 53, 54, 58, 59, 68, 69, 70, 76, 80, 81, 83; concept of, 4; consolidation, 8-9; crisis, 9-10, 11; formation, 4-5, 8, 10; social vs. spiritual, 53-56
Inner life, 56

Jacobson, E., 5
James, Alice (1848-92), 36, 43-44, *111*
James, Catharine Barber (third wife of William of Albany), 15
James, Garth Wilkinson (1845-83), 38, 115
James, Henry, Jr. (1843-1916), 73, 74, 78, *107, 109;* born, 36; Boston visit, 25; description of childhood, 39; ill with typhus, 45
James, Henry, Sr. (1811-82), *frontispiece,* 1, 2, 14, 15, 16, 72, 78, *93;* absence of paternal influence, 19; abuse of father's funds, 24-25; and Ralph Waldo Emerson, 30-31; and Thomas Carlyle, 32-34, 35; attention to William's moral development, scientific potential, 45, 47-48; battle with morality, 40; burned, 19; *Church of Christ Not an Ecclesiasticism, A Letter to a Sectarian, The,* 41; closeness to mother, 20; concept of consciousness, 56-59, 61; cut off in will, 27; defends his ideas, 68-69; departs for Europe (1837), 29; develops identity as theological writer, 49;

drinking problem, 23; early childhood, 18–22; early influence of ministers, 21; Europe (1855–58), 42–47; fled to Boston, 25; ideas, 49–62; identity accepted by William, 79–83; inner world, 49–50; *Lectures and Miscellanies*, 55; leaves Princeton, 29; leg amputated, 19; life in Boston, 26; marriage and early family years, 35–42; meets the devil, 34, 35; *Nature of Evil, The*, 41; preoccupation with security, 42; relationship with father, 20; relationship with wife, Mary, 36; religious conversion, 34, 35, 75–76; *Remarks on the Apostolic Gospel*, 30; resistance to William's scientific interests, 78; returns family to U.S. (1860), 47–48; returns to Albany (1845), 36; returns to Europe (1843), 32; returns to Europe (1855), 41; returns to Union College, 26–27; schooling of children, 39, 42–43; *Secret of Swedenborg, The*, 58, 73; self-expression, 50–53; *Society the Redeemed Form of Man*, 61; student at Princeton, 28; theology formed, 29–30; theory of spontaneous action, 51–52; to Windsor (1844), 33; turns to science, 31; view of creation, 55

James, Henry III, *frontispiece*, 78
James, Mary Walsh (wife of Henry, Sr.), 35–36, 95
James, Robert (son of William of Albany), 16
James, Robertson (Bob) (1846–1910), 38, *113*
James, William (of Albany) (1771–1832), 19, 20, *91;* American success, 13–18; arrived in America, 13; died, 27; financial genius, 55; marriages, 15; obituary, 27; sensitivity to his children, 22; widowerhood, 14–15; will, 27–28; will broken, 28
James, William (half-brother of Henry, Sr.), 16; begins theological research, 28; cut off in will, 27; graduates from Princeton, 28
James, William (1842–1910), 1, 2, *97, 99, 101, 103, 105, 107, 109;* acceptance of Henry, Sr.'s identity, 79–83; acceptance of own unhappiness, 73; ambivalence about career, 78; appointed physiology instructor at Harvard (1872), 78; as replacement for William of Albany, 62; backaches begin, 64; begins study of psychology, 72; born, 36; confronts Henry, Sr.'s views, 66–67, 69–70; convalescent trip to Europe (1867), 65; defense of father's ideas, 83; enters medical school, 64; European travel (1873), 78; expedition to Brazil, 64; growing interest in art, 46; growing interest in science, 45–46; hypochondria, 66, 72, 74, 78; inability to become his father's philosophical heir, 67; leaves for Harvard (1861), 63; *Literary Remains of the Late Henry James, The*, 79, 81; moral development, 47; relationship with brothers, 46; renounces art, 48; returns to Cambridge (1868), 72; suicidal fantasies, 65–66; terrifying image, 75; terrifying image and Henry, Sr.'s religious conversion compared, 75–76; *Varieties of Religious Experience, The*, 75, 76; views of Henry, Sr.'s philosophy, 70
Janick, A., and S. Toulman, 6
Jenks family, 26

La Forge, John, 46
Lectures and Miscellanies (Henry James, Sr.), 55
Letters on Theron and Aspasio (Robert Sandeman), 30
Lifton, R. J., 5
Literary Remains of the Late Henry James, The (William James), 79, 81
Love, creator's infinite, 58–60
Luther, Martin, 7–9

Mazlish, B., 6
McIntyre, Archibald, 24–25
Moral development, 46, 47, 80
Morality, 52, 60–61
Morse, Jedidiah, 13

Nature of Evil, The (Henry James, Sr.), 41
New Times (journal), 37
North American Review, 65
Nott, Dr. Eliphalet, 16–18, 23; influence on Henry, Sr., 23–24

Original sin, doctrine of, 21

Pain, 52, 62
Perry, R. B., 16, 65
Princeton University, 28
Psychohistory, 1, 3–6; Erikson's theory of, 3–12
Psychological: determinism, 77; understanding applied to biography, 1

Rapaport, D. A., 3, 4
Relationships, 2, 5, 35, 38, 43, 49, 51, 53, 54, 57, 59, 60, 61, 62, 71, 73, 78, 80; experience of, 56–62; sponsoring, 9–11
Remarks on the Apostolic Gospel (Henry James, Sr.), 30

Renouvier, Charles, 77
Rosenzweig, S., 6

Sandeman, Robert, 29-30; *Letters on Theron and Aspasio*, 30
Schafer, R., 5
Science, 31-32
Secret of Swedenborg, The (Henry James, Sr.), 58, 73
Self-expression, 49, 50-53
Socialism, 36, 38
Society the Redeemed Form of Man (Henry James, Sr.), 61
Sponsorship, 1, 6, 9-11; paternal, 14, 18
Spontaneity, 49, 51, 52, 55, 57, 59, 60
Stout, C., 6
Swedenborg, Emanuel, 35, 36

Union College, 16-18, 22, 23, 24

Van Rensselaer, Stephen, 41
Varieties of Religious Experience, The (William James), 75, 76
Vulnerability, 10, 43, 52, 53, 60, 62, 76

Ward, Tom, 64, 71, 72, 73, 76-77
Weld, Isaac, Jr., 13
Wyman, Jeffries, 64

Yates and McIntyre (lawyers), 16-17, 24-25
Young, F. H., 29
Young Man Luther (E. H. Erikson), 6